x2n

Tricia : many happy
returns of the days,
with love from
Vicky & John
January 10
1978

The Butterfly Lions

*Lion-dog on a bamboo stump,
blue chalcedony*

RUMER GODDEN

The Butterfly Lions

THE STORY OF THE PEKINGESE
IN HISTORY, LEGEND AND ART

M

ISBN 0 333 21746 2

First published 1977 by
MACMILLAN LONDON LIMITED
*4 Little Essex Street London WC2R 3LF
and Basingstoke
Associated companies in New York Dublin
Melbourne Johannesburg and Delhi*

*Printed in Great Britain by William Clowes & Sons Limited
London, Beccles and Colchester*

Contents

To the memory of Mrs (Clarice) Ashton Cross, from 1905 onward doyenne of the pekingese world in the West, and whose instinct and skill did so much to establish the breed in its present standard of soundness and beauty; also to her daughter, Miss Cynthia, my friend and counsellor and from whom almost all my pekingese have come; she has given me hours, days, weeks, months, years of pleasure and also taught me the valuable lesson that such pleasure has to be paid for with hard work and concern.

Introduction

This is not a 'dog' book in the sense that it will tell anyone how to choose, look after and breed pekingese; since 1905 there have been several such, written with knowledge, love and understanding. *The Butterfly Lions* could be called a romance – except that it happens to be true, or as true as research and the many scholars who have helped me can make it; I have tried to separate fact and legend. It is an attempt to trace the story of the pekingese from antiquity to the present day. 'They all have long histories', the Dowager Empress of China told her lady-in-waiting, but even she did not know how long.

Nor did I – until I began.

Years ago, on my sixteenth birthday, I was given five pounds to buy a Persian kitten. Most girls pine for an animal of their own but, even as a little child, for me the longing was not just for an animal but for an extraordinary animal; I would have loved a unicorn rather than a pony, if there had really been unicorns, or a salamander, or a kylin – that mythical monster with a head of a lion and the body of a dragon – if I had known about them, but a Persian kitten was the nearest my dear family could come to fulfilling this unusual wish.

In the pet shop there was a rusty old bird-cage and in it sat a puppy, small, square, black with cream paws and vest; he was of a kind I had not seen before, but his eyes, that took up most of his face, looked at me compellingly. I bought him, my five pounds was accepted as a down-payment with a pledge of half a crown a week from my allowance for a year.

I am sure now that the shopkeeper did not expect me to come back as, in pekingese parlance, this puppy was flawed; for one thing his lower jaw protruded, a fault the Chinese call 'earth covers heaven', so that he was worth precisely nothing – to anybody else; but I am glad now that I met every one of those Saturday morning extortions so that my lifetime of pekingese – I have had more than twenty – was founded on fidelity, however slight. I called the puppy Piers because it was the most aristocratic name I could think of.

In those days, though I had an ignoramus's love of things Chinese, poetry, ceramics and paintings, I knew nothing of the dynasties and their emperors and empresses; of palace cities and paeony-terraced ten-mile-wide gardens; of eunuchs and concubines; of the silk caravan route or of opium clippers. I knew practically nothing either of Queen Victoria and Court life at Windsor, Balmoral and Buckingham Palace; of treaties and wars and, if I had, would not have dreamed of connecting them with pekingese. I only knew Piers but my instinct was right – no matter how flawed, Piers by origin was aristocratic – more, he was Imperial.

It may seem absurd to link a race of small dogs with two vast empires, one Western, the other Far Eastern and, in particular, with the two powerful women who, in the nineteenth century, ruled over them, but no one can follow the story of the pekingese without some knowledge of these two utterly different and distant worlds.

The Chinese regarded Westerners as vandals and there is certainly something unthinking and prejudiced in the image of this blithe and historic breed we have conjured up and, sadly, often made fact: that of rich ladies' lapdogs, pampered and delicate, dressed in coats, bad-tempered, even snappy, wheezing, snoring and so adipose they can only waddle. If they have been distorted into this, the fault lies with the owner, not with the dog. True, elderly people buy them believing they need little exercise — which is wrong; most pekingese detest laps, are even wary of fondling, are only bad-tempered through being made liverish from too many tidbits. It is true, too, that they snore, but that is because of what man, through the ages, has done to their noses, and the snores are usually only a soporific snuffle.

The author's miniature Jade Button of Alderbourne

As for waddling! Pekingese can race, even hurdle; they retrieve, swim and are more hardy than many a big dog, walking in any weather; sometimes in snow or deluging rain my pekingese have been the only dogs out in the woods or on the hills.

Most of us dog-owners are ordinary people and so most pekingese nowadays have to settle not for palaces, but for an ordinary humdrum life, but they still treat it in a lordly way. Piers, for instance, soon became a well-known character in our Sussex town. 'In quod again', a policeman would come to our door and say, and I would have to go to the police station and redeem Piers with a fine of five shillings. The trouble was that while I was away at school he was bored and so would slip out, and kind people, seeing a small pekingese wandering alone, thought he was lost. By no means: a bus ran from a stop near our then house up to the Downs; one morning I caught it with Piers, meaning to take him for a walk on the rolling green hills – it should have been a chariot or imperial cart or, at least, a car, but for us it had to be a bus. 'That your dog, Miss?' asked the conductor. 'Well, I guess you owe the Corporation at least five pounds.' It seems that Piers caught the bus in the morning, took himself up to the front seat on top – buses were open-topped then – alighted at the terminus at the foot of the Downs and went rabbitting and, at the right time, caught the bus home. I had long been puzzled by the earth on his paws and ruff.

He became my shadow, mourning if I went anywhere without him, making a carnival of joy of my return; alert to every word I said, sensitive to every mood, but after twenty halcyon months we went back to India and I had to leave him. I never saw him again.

'Let no one enter lightly on a Chinese dog. They make themselves too beloved', says the proverb and it is true; unlike the Empress Tzŭ-hsi, I have strayed from my allegiance and had dogs of other breeds – and loved them – but there was a difference and when, ten years after Piers I was given my second pekingese, I knew that these dogs, and only these, fulfilled that strange longing that has always haunted me.

Pekingese are not as other dogs – just as goldfish are not as other fish; as Ellic Howe says in his *Pekingese Scrapbook,* 'they represent something both intriguing and mysterious.' It is not only that their ways are different, they have a fastidiousness that shows for instance in their recoil from any meat that is slightly high, whereas other dogs, finding a long-dead rabbit or bird, will go and roll in it. Pekingese are distressed at having a flea or if they are dirty; they do not damage flowerbeds beyond the inevitable leg-lifting, and are the only puppies I know that pull daisies and play with them. They are different too in their wilfulness and their independence – Piers carried his like a banner; in fact, there is in them something untouched, even aloof – probably the last thing most owners would want in a dog. Perhaps it is this aloofness of spirit that makes some people say they are cats; certainly not – they are pekingese, a connoisseur's dog and, over the years, I hope I have learned a little, though only a little, of what it means to be a connoisseur.

In this attempt to tell the history and show the background of these butterfly-lions, there is nothing new, only what I have gathered from books, mostly rare and out of print, from letters and diaries, old records and, more abundantly, from Chinese art: from what learned people have been kind enough to teach me and from my own conclusions which are probably iconoclastic, but then I make no claim to authority. I simply wrote this small history for the same reason I keep my pekingese – for pleasure.

The Chinese

Dynasties

Ming	*1368 – 1644*
Ch'ing	*1644 – 1912*

Emperors of the Ch'ing (Manchu) Dynasty	*1644 – 1912*
Shun-chih	*1644 – 1661*
K'ang-hsi	*1662 – 1722*
Yung-chêng	*1723 – 1735*
Ch'ien-lung	*1736 – 1795*
Chia-ch'ing	*1796 – 1821*
Tao-kuang	*1821 – 1850*
Hsien-fêng	*1851 – 1861*
T'ung-chih	*1862 – 1873*
Kuang-hsü	*1874 – 1907*
Hsüan-t'ung	*1908 – 1912*

ONCE UPON A TIME a lioness grew tired of the brute attentions of her mate and yielded to the delicate caresses of a butterfly; (if you have ever been given a butterfly kiss, someone else's eye-lashes fluttering against your cheek, you will know how delicately teasing that is). The result of this mating was a pekingese and ever afterwards these little dogs have to be as brave as lions and dainty as butterflies. (A version of this legend is also told in Africa but there the one who fell in love with the butterfly — a female — was the lion and the love was never consummated.)

CHAPTER ONE

'Golden-coated nimble dogs'

On 2 March 1872, there was a royal death at Windsor Castle; no flags were lowered, no mourning was ordered, no headlines appeared in the press but the death, though small, was royal. Her Majesty, Queen Victoria, might have been told of it after she had finished her breakfast. 'Ma'am, word has been sent from the Windsor kennels that Lootie has died.'

'Lootie?' One imagines that the famous blue eyes, slightly prominent and paler now, stared uncertainly. 'Lootie?'

'Yes, Ma'am, the little Chinese dog from the Summer Palace at Peking.'

'She has died?'

'Last night, ma'am.'

'She has lived a long time. It must be eleven years since she came and she could have been four or five years old then. Sixteen is old for a dog.'

'Yes Ma'am, but this was a pekingese.'

Lootie, a fawn and white pekingese, came to the winter castle, as Windsor in 1861 could certainly have been described,

humanity; to them it was a dog, but a dog that had become, in its small way, divine.

The myths surrounding its origin give an inkling of this divinity – no other breed has myths in its ancestry; though it may sound a fairytale, a myth arises from a reason, perhaps characteristics. Besides the lion and butterfly legend told on page 14 there is another about pekingese origin, in fact it is more commonly told; it is of a marmoset which fell in love with a lion. Being so diminutive, her passion could not be consummated, and she was in such a state of wretchedness that the gods took pity on her and, in some versions, made her big enough, in others the lion small enough, for the marriage to take place. Again, the result was a pekingese and, while the story is phylogenetically impossible, it is true that many pekingese have marmoset traits; the Manchu Empress Tzŭ-hsi, in the 'pearls' of wisdom she is supposed to have written about pekingese, laid down that their noses 'be like that of the Hindu monkey god', i.e. flat – and some do have monkey faces – but these usually do not have the sweetness of character shown by those of the wider 'flower' or 'pansy' masks – a pekingese face is called a mask – those of monkey masks are inclined to be spiteful. Properly trained pekingese are uncommonly agile as the photograph of Tai-Tu hurdling, on page 157, shows. Most are as mischievous as any monkey and they often like fruit, even tangerines, which is unusual in a dog; but whether the myth is of a butterfly or monkey, there is always a lion.

In the early days of China, the tiger was the royal beast but, with the spread of Buddhism the lion ousted him because he was more than royal – a spirit – and in over fifteen hundred years of history the lion has found an 'aspect' or small echo of this divinity in the pekingese.

Just as we, in the West, have Sirius the dog star, the ancient

Chinese had celestial dogs among the stars. Their term for an eclipse is the 'eating up' by a dog of the sun or moon, and during an eclipse the people used to go out with gongs and drums and incense to try and frighten the Tien Kow, or 'heavenly dog', from his meal. There appears to have been another dog in the sky, the Barking Dog, 'which had the size of an elephant and the likeness of an owl and eats its parents. Its head is of brass, its neck of iron; terrible in battle, its antagonist is consumed even to the last of its bones.' This heavenly – or horrible – dog had the power to snatch children from their houses – one can imagine peasant mothers and nurses frightening children into quaking goodness by it. The stories are confused and both may have been based on the mythical monster dog Fu.

There were other dog superstitions. In Peking there used to be a temple dedicated to the god Erh Lang who, like St George, is the slayer of dragons, and he is the master of that Tien Kow, 'the dog that howls in the sky'. For this reason, anyone who owned a treasured dog would put a miniature of it in clay, brass, silver, jade or ivory on Erh Lang's altar to protect the pet from harm; I hope I am not usually a covetous person but I have seen three of these 'images', so small that they had to be looked at through a magnifying glass. They were only of brass but exquisitely carved and, if I could, I would have stolen them! These star beliefs and celestial dogs, though, have nothing to do with the evolution of the pekingese.

There are scrolls of pekingese, not written but painted; the most lifelike belongs to the time of the Tao-Kuang period, 1821-1850 which could be called the heyday or golden age of the pekingese in China. The scroll is lettered 'After Tsou Yi Kwei, K'ang-hsi period, 1662–1722', so that evidently earlier painted scrolls were also dog books, but this one is especially beautiful: a hundred little dogs playing, fighting,

The scroll of a hundred pekingese dogs

sleeping among blossom and chrysanthemum flowers.

Another, of the Empress Tzŭ-hsi's time – its date is 1890 – is the work of her Instructress of Painting; these were the stud-books of the Imperial dogs, but the scroll of Chinese dog history unrolls far further back, beyond Confucius or any thought of Buddhism to the Chou dynasty, about 1000 B.C., when 'square dogs' were exacted as part of the tribute from the southern states. To be part of a tribute is proof that they were valuable but there is nothing to show whether they were large or small, yet in the sixth century B.C., Confucius, trying to instil economy, wrote that 'the discarded hangings of a chariot may be used to wrap the beloved saddle horse for burial and the torn chariot umbrella will serve to cover the dear house dog in his grave', and Chinese umbrellas, even chariot ones, were not large. In the same period it is recorded that after a day's sport the larger dogs followed the chariots but the smaller, 'those having short mouths', i.e. flat faces, were carried in carts.

In the first century A.D., a little more can be learned in support of this theory, in that these short-mouthed dogs were called 'pai' or 'under the table' dogs. Chinese tables were low, the people round them sitting on mats, so these dogs must have been short-legged as well as short-mouthed – in fact, only eight to ten inches high. As V. W. F. Collier says in his scholarly book, *Dogs of China and Japan in Nature and Art*, it is from such small sentences that a description of pekingese ancestry has literally to be 'gleaned'.

More vivid still are the extremely old and rare modelled or sculptured small statues of these dogs, usually 'grave' images, that were entombed with the dead so that they should have company in their lonely pilgrimage.

Of pottery or stone, some go back to the Han dynasty and

Grave images
Above: date uncertain
Right: 9th—10th century A.D.

Below: 'The long-neck dog', a grotesque in Ch'ang Sha style

are pekingese in many characteristics – short legs, 'cobby' bodies, feathered tails but not necessarily the flat face; this, one imagines, is because they belong to an era before Buddhism came to China after which these little pet dogs were bred to resemble as closely as possible the 'spirit' lion. Yet flat faces were known; the earliest documented figure of a 'short-mouthed' dog is the curious one reproduced on page 25, Han period, of brown glazed pottery, Ch'ang Sha style; though it has prick ears and the curious long neck – probably abnormally elongated to fit the artist's sense of humour – the face, with its round eyes, wide mouth and flattened nose, is clearly a fore-runner of pekingese, as is the body, even the body's pose. I wish Mr Collier could have seen it. The beautiful little chariot ornament of the same period, though resembling a windblown pekingese cannot be authenticated.

Though dogs are, of all creatures, the most genetically adaptable to their breeders' wishes – see how quickly most breeds have been evolved or altered – pekingese seem as wilful in this as in anything else and, up to the T'ang dynasty nosed pekingese can be clearly seen in paintings, ceramics and jade – and are often very unattractive. They do not easily conform to wishes or theories; a miniature bitch bred to a miniature dog can still have a full-sized pup: a coloured coat can appear in what was hoped was a pure white strain* and, even today, some unfortunate little creatures can suddenly revert to the disgrace of a small, but distinct, nose.

By the seventeenth century though, only flat faces were esteemed as can be seen by the paintings on scrolls, fans, and screens of this period; it is rare to find paintings of dogs in any period before this time, though those that we know of often

---

* There seems to have been a separate or albino strain of white pekingese in old China, but these had the albino characteristics of pink skin in eyelids and noses; the whites of modern breed are not albino.

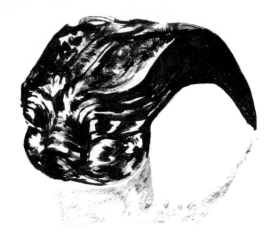

Above: Han chariot
ornament
Right: Monster mask
from Yi-hsien-Hopei
(See page 33)

have the subtitle 'after so-and-so', giving the name of a far earlier artist. Pekingese also appear on the snuff bottles so loved by the Chinese.

But, looking backward, both art and history tell us clearly that small pet dogs were extant and treasured in China at least from the Han dynasty; also that they were Imperial. It is, for instance, fact that the Emperor Ling Ti who ruled from A.D. 168–190, had such an obsession with his favourite little dog that he gave him the official 'hat' of the most important literary grade of the time, equivalent of a present-day Nobel prize; as the hat was more than eight inches high and ten inches broad not much could have been seen of the dog! Its companions in the Palace were given the rank of viceroy, the bitches taking the rank of their wives. The book describing this adds with Chinese gravity 'This had the effect of likening high officials to dogs and was bad practice.'

Ling Ti was one of the 'madcap' monarchs as the historians called them, but there were others almost as silly. In A.D. 565, the Emperor Kao-Wei of the Northern Chou dynasty gave the name of Ch'ih Hu, or 'red tiger', to a certain Persian dog. He also gave it the rank and privileges of Chun Chun (closely allied to those of a duke). The dog was fed with the choicest meat and rice. It was granted the revenue of a prefecture. When the Emperor was mounted the dog rode upon a mat placed in front of the saddle. It must have been small to ride in front of its master in this way and, though described as Persian, was possibly one of the short-mouthed dogs of North China. The Empress Tzŭ-hsi always said pekingese came from the North though, as we have seen, there were short-mouthed dogs in the South.

It seems definite that the Northern variety were mingled with at least one European strain, the Maltese. When the

Roman Empire broke up Malta became part of Turkoman, and Caius, physician to Queen Elizabeth I, travelling there, wrote of the Turks 'that the dogs have no especial masters except the very little tiny Maltese'. These were the silky toy spaniels seen in many old paintings and called by Doctor Caius 'comfort dogs' or 'the comforter', as they were small enough to be carried in the bosom or laid on the stomach to ease pain. The pekingese would hardly rank as a 'comfort dog', it is too independent to relish being carried and would have hated to lie on anyone's stomach. Caius also mentions another 'highbred dog' from the island of Melita in the Sicilian Straits. It, too, was 'very little tiny . . .', 'the smaller . . . the more pleasing it is'. These miniature creatures probably found their way to China in the silk caravans but, long before this, in the reign of the Emperor Kou Tzŭ (618–629) there was sent from Byzantium or, as it had become, Constantinople, a gift of two dogs, a male and a female, to the Chinese Court. Their height was six tsun (about seven and a half inches) and their length one ch'ih (about a foot). They were of 'great intelligence and could lead horses by the reins' – they must also have had great authority for such minute creatures to do this! 'And each was trained to light its master's path at night by carrying a torch in its mouth.' Severe training when one remembers the torches were aflame!

These dogs were born in the Fu-lin country and for many years small pet dogs were called Fulins: in fact, the pekingese has had many names: Fu-lins; Hai-pah or Hai-pai – sometimes spelt Hai-bah – which simply means lapdogs; Pai; Dragon dog and, of course, Lion dog; Pekin palace dog; 'Sleeve'; while even the artist Katharine Carl, who should have known better as she was allowed to live in the Summer Palace while painting the Empress Tzŭ-hsi's portrait and was

actually given a pekingese, called it a 'Peking Pug', as the Empress's lady-in-waiting, Princess Der-ling, persisted in doing though corrected by the Empress herself. (There were, of course, pugs in China; it was from China that they came to Europe; especially Holland, but even in early times their description was quite different, being smooth-coated, tails in a tight curl and having small ears the size of 'half a dried apricot'.)

Before Dr Caius, another traveller – one Harrison, quoted by V. W. F. Collier – had remarked in 1588 that, if 'the little dogs had a hole in the forepart of their heads, the better they are accepted.' This is probably the first European reference to the deep 'stop' above the flat nose or nostrils of the true pekingese.

There are many 'short-dog' stories of the T'ang dynasty, of which the most famous is of the Emperor Ming (A.D. 718–755), who had a favourite wife, as beautiful as she was tactful, and who owned an equally beautiful and tactful dog, Wo. One day, the Emperor was playing chess with a fellow prince and, seeing that her Lord was to be defeated – an unthinkable indignity even in a game – the wife whispered to Wo, who immediately jumped up on the board so that the pieces were upset and the match ruined to the great delight of the unsporting Emperor – and probably the relief of his opponent. It seems possible that it was this Wo who is named in the couplet written by the poet Yuan Wei Chih.

How fierce is proud Wo
Though still in his slumbers . . . .

but Wo was yet another name for the whole race of small dogs.
An especially Imperial dog was T'ao Hua – Peach Flower –

Dogs coupling, watched by court ladies

given to the Emperor T'ai-tsung of the Sung dynasty some-
where about A.D. 990.
It again was:

> extremely small and very intelligent. It followed the
> Emperor everywhere but when they went into the Hall
> of Audience it changed places and walked in front so
> that it could announce the arrival of its Imperial
> Master. T'ai-tsung fell ill and the dog refused to eat;
> when the Emperor died it manifested its sorrow with
> tears and whining. The palace eunuchs tried to train
> Peach Flower to precede the new Emperor into Audience
> but without success, so the newcomer gracefully bowed
> out and caused an iron cage to be made with white
> cushions as a sign of mourning and this, containing
> the dog, was carried in the Imperial chair to his
> master's tomb. There the dog died.

One cannot say with certainty that these early dogs were
pekingese and yet all the tales emphasise the same characteristics, even echo the same words: intelligence, dexterity,
courage, the devotion they gave even to death, and the potency
of the devotion they inspired in their owners – as they still do
today – and which seems to go deeper than usual even among
the almost fanatically dog-minded English. Mrs Patrick
Campbell, for instance, could have salved her great acting
career had she consented to come back to England from
America, but she would not, because it meant parting from
her pekingese Moonbeam, who would have had to go into
quarantine, and 'the grand old man of the museums and fine
arts', as The Times called Sir Karl Parker of the Ashmolean
Museum and the National Gallery, a sane man if ever there
were one, refused a tempting assignment in Venice, one of the

great loves of his life, because of another great love – his pekingese 'who [again] would not have enjoyed the spells of quarantine on his return'.

Then too there is that continual phrase 'short-mouthed', which surely must mean without a dog's usual pointed nose? and 'under the table', which, as has been seen, gives a sure indication of size.

There is a bronze monster mask and ring p'u shou excavated at Yi-hsien Hopei founded, as far as scholarship can tell, on the dragon kuei, a mythical beast, yet, if one looks at it carefully, the mask and the ring combine so that the whole is not unlike a little dog with featherings and big eyes, a wide mouth below a flat nose and wrinkle, an extra long tongue joining the mask to a feathered ruff; the date is fifth century B.C., more than a thousand years before the long tongue became fashionable in pekingese breeding and probably this is an iconoclastic fancy, but it could not have been impossible for that long-ago bronze worker to have seen a 'short-mouthed' dog. The windblown head of the Han dynasty, too, is clearly not a Fu dog – the monsters that guard tombs, temples, gates and pavilion roofs. Perhaps the pekingese race is older than we think.

Buddhism came to China from India and, though there are traces back to the first century A.D., it was not adopted as the state religion until the fifth and sixth centuries. The lion was Buddha's vehicle and his familiar; it could become so large it could fill the sky, but usually Buddha rode on its back if he wished to travel. He could also and conveniently cause it to shrink to such smallness that he could carry it in the sleeve of his robe.

There are two types of this dog/lion (which museums usually list as 'lions') that are often called kylins, but the kylin was a mythical monster having the body of a dragon and the head of a lion; it was supposed to appear only once in ten thousand years. The pure Buddhist type of Fu dog has no embellishments of harness, no ball or cub under its paw, while the Lamaistic dog/lions that filtered into China from the North were more elaborate; in these the ball, which often looks embroidered, represents the sun, while the cub was under the mother's paw because the Chinese believed her milk came through her pads. All Fu dogs, however, are similar and, though they have more than a touch of the dragon, if one looks at them carefully, at the big eyes, (though exaggerated to goggles), the flat face, the wide-mouthed, flat head, the fringes and mane, the tail curved over the back, they might be grotesque caricatures of the pekingese. The Fu manes and fringes are usually curly whereas a pekingese should be straight-coated; in fact, the lamas were later so embarrassed by their lion's twisted curls that they invented a legend that Buddha remained so long in motionless contemplation that snails crawled over his lion's head.

One must remember that few Chinese, or Tibetan, artists had ever seen a lion, though the emperors, particularly during the Yuan dynasty, kept them in menageries. Marco Polo in his travels saw lions 'roaming in the Palace courtyards', when he visited Kublai Khan who had conquered all China, gradually making it into an empire that stretched from Korea to Arabia and East Poland, putting an end to the Sung dynasties and establishing the Mongol or Yuan in 1280. The Great Khan made Peking the capital and, being a convert to Lamaistic Buddhism, attached importance to the 'spirit lion'. His menagerie lions must have been stunted because Marco Polo continues, 'These beasts were small and short of body', but he endorses their affinity with pet dogs by adding, 'They are as-

Fu dog in green jade

tonishingly like the golden-coated nimble dogs which the people bred in their homes.'

Evidently in those days, though favourites of emperors, the little dogs were not exclusively royal, as there is another reference of this time – the thirteenth century – to a civilian who bred a Chin Ssu – literally 'golden silk' dog in his house. It was not more than a foot long and when guests were present it lay under the table. Once again the story of its intelligence and fidelity is told; its owner fell ill and, in sympathy, the dog refused to eat. When the master died, it beat its head against the coffin so violently that it too died.

This is one of the few civilian stories of pekingese but, under the Emperor Wan Li (1536–1620), a certain eunuch named Tu secretly kept a small 'hai-ba' or 'pai' dog in his home. This came to the ears of the chief eunuch of the Board of Punishment who threatened to tell the Emperor but was bought off by Tu with a thousand silver taels. It must have been one of the most expensive dogs in history.

The Ming emperors of this time though seem to have preferred cats – their palaces were over-run with them – but in 1644, the Manchus conquered Peking, swiftly making the whole of China into one great empire, and the little palace dogs, rare and important as they had been, took on a new dignity.

Coming from the North, the Ch'ing or Manchu emperors brought with them the Lamaistic form of Buddhism long followed in Tibet – and by Kublai Khan – and which laid great emphasis on the spirit lion. The people were encouraged to observe these traditions and, as the Emperor to them was the Son of Heaven, the Buddha, he needed his lion – not merely a 'spirit' or symbolic lion but a tangible one, and this led to 'a slight difficulty'.

Lion-dog, detail from a painting of a female immortal

By an oversight of nature no lions were forthcoming [in China]. The priests had to see what could be done; first of all they did their best to find out what a lion was like. Fortunately there were plenty of images [those Fu dogs and chimeras] some imported from India, showing a broad-headed creature with a massive front tapering to lighter hindquarters; a big mouth, fierce protruding eyes and powerful fore-paws. More remarkable still, the creature was shown with a shaggy growth of mane over the shoulders and thick tufts of coarse hair over the elbows and at the end of the tail. Assuredly none of the larger animals available in China was capable of passing for a lion.

But at the Chinese court there was to be found a great variety of small dogs . . . which bore a sufficient resemblance to the images of the Buddhist lion to pass muster. The priests came to a hasty decision and at once collected those specimens of the Pekingese dog that showed the most marked lion-like attributes.

'Where is my lion?' enquired the Emperor impatiently . . . 'Unless I get that lion quickly somebody's head will come off.'

'Omnipotence,' replied a trembling functionary, 'there is already a good supply of lions in the palace.'

'Then produce them,' said the Emperor, and forthwith the little Lion Dog made his entry upon the stage of world history. For a moment, no doubt, his fate hung in the balance whilst the priests explained his points of resemblance to the images imported . . . and found plausible reasons for his lack of size, which rendered this Chinese lion unsuitable for riding. But in the end the Son of Heaven was satisfied. He had his lion.

That is a flight of imagination but behind the whimsicality – it is supposed to be told by a pekingese dog – lies truth in that the relationship between the true or 'spirit lion' and the lion-dog came from a Tibetan sacred writing which begins 'In the West there was a Buddha named Manjusri'.

'There was a Buddha named Manjusri'. This may seem confusing but Buddha had many 'aspects' or 'avatars' of which Manjusri, God of Learning, was one. Manjusri was always accompanied by a small 'hah-pah' (lap) dog as he travelled the four continents in the disguise of a simple priest, carrying his 'lion' in his sleeve.

On his travels he one day met a Taoist who begged him to obtain for him an audience with Manjusri. The Buddha invited the Taoist to accompany him to his home. When the Taoist had taken tea and rice, he again requested the Buddha to secure for him a vision of Manjusri. The Buddha told him that he must observe his vows with great strictness and that Manjusri would then be manifested to him. On this the Taoist, bursting into anger, cried vehemently, 'I am indeed keeping my vows. If not, why should I have come hither to see the Buddha?' Then said the Buddha, 'If this be verily so,

Japanese embroidery of a black and white pekingese among rose petals

look up into the sky'. The Taoist raised his head and perceived in the sky a glow of five-coloured light together with clouds of five colours. In the heavens he saw the 'hah-pah' dog transformed into a mighty lion with the Buddha riding upon his back.

The Tibetans too, bred a race of small dogs as living representatives of the Buddha's dog-lion, the shih-tzu – 'shih' means 'lion' – but they were never adopted as its actual symbol, nor had they the refinement of the pekingese; though endearing they are woolly, not silken, and could be called the peasant equivalent of the palace dog. The Dalai Lama of the time brought some when he visited the Empress Tzŭ-hsi in the 1900s. Pugs, as we have seen, also came from China and the Japanese spaniel or ch'in is obviously related to the pekingese but with its slenderness and spindly legs soon lost all connection with the lion. In fact there are several claims, but one claim is certain: with the coming of the Ch'ing emperors, the pekingese dog, almost in the form we know it now, became the small and sacred lion, so sacred that people outside, even of noble blood, were not allowed to set eyes on them; even the palace servants – except for the dog eunuchs – had to turn away their heads if they met one of these imperial small beings.

It was probably under the most sensitive and scholarly of all the Ch'ing emperors, Ch'ien-lung, father-in-law of the Empress Tzŭ-hsi, that these little dogs were given the name by which we know them now – Peiching Kou or Pekingese.

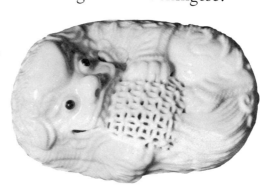

White porcelain figure of a puppy with a ball

CHAPTER TWO

Empresses-in-Waiting

That small Chinese morsel of life, Lootie, a pekingese bitch, was not only the first of her breed to come to the West as far as documents can disclose – others had started the voyage but had not survived – but she was the first thread linking the courts of two great women, Queen Victoria and the Empress Tzŭ-hsi, counterparts ruling vast empires but, at that time, wrapped in cocoons of ignorance or misconception about one another's countries and subjects.

To reach China from Europe had always taken months, even years; as late as the 1860s, the journey, by sea, could last four months; if a ship had steam as well as sail, like the paddle-wheel frigate *Odin* or the transport *Bosphorus* in which Lootie travelled – both ships figure in the pekingese story – only enough coal could be carried to use steam for entering or leaving port or negotiating difficult channels and rivers. No wonder then that China, to most Westerners, was still Cathay, a fabulous and faraway land of flowery fables and curious customs that, to the European mind, were topsy-turvy while, to the Chinese, who knew of no other empire but their own, Britain was a small island, an appendage of Holland, and filled with hairy barbarians who, though so far away, were still vassals of the Emperor of China, the Son of Heaven. Yet, for the last half of the nineteenth century, the lives of the English and Chinese queens were parallels. What a pity that they could not have met, have talked together and exchanged their reminiscences so like – and unlike – one another's.

China, from centuries before Christ, had been noted for her silks, so that Lootie could be called a silken thread. Though long-legged compared to pekingese of the twentieth century and more close-coated, she was silken-furred as can be seen by her portrait that hangs now in the Lord Chamberlain's office – it used to be in Windsor Castle.

In the painting her miniature size is shown by the nosegay of flowers at her feet; she has the large lustrous eyes laid down for pekingese by the Empress Tzŭ-hsi, eyes that can eloquently plead, and the white blaze down her forehead, with the small white spot below it, signifies rank, the jade button in front of the hat of a mandarin or high official, though not of the highest rank which was a ruby button. This mark in pekingese lore means good luck.

There was no luck for Lootie; in all the books and diaries of the Opium War and the many that have been written about pekingese, describing her capture and arrival in England, not one writer has given a thought to the feelings of this little creature. During the two days of the sacking and burning of the Summer Palace, everything Lootie knew and trusted had been destroyed; she was deserted – her royal owners had fled. There was gunfire – pekingese are shocked by, and abhor, loud noises; even the, to Lootie and her palace companions, familiar Chinese New Year fire-crackers, must have been terrifying. There would have been horrible smells of blood, smoke, putrid flesh – dogs live by smell. She must have under-

Lootie

gone rough handling as Captain Hart Dunne did not himself find her in the Summer Palace but bought her in the French camp, as he tells in his diary:

> I have been able to retain a good many trifles that I bought there [the French camp], also a pretty little dog, smaller than any King Charles, a real Chinese sleeve dog. It has silver bells round its neck. People say, [he added], it is the most perfect little beauty they have ever seen.

But still a 'trifle'. Pekingese are the most affectionate of dogs, the most home-attached; if, to the outside world, they often seem aloof, it is because of this deep attachment, and Lootie, in her abandonment, must have attached herself to the young Captain and he to her; why else, on the long voyage, did she sleep in his forage cap? Yet, in April 1861, he wrote to the Keeper of the Privy Purse:

> Captain Hart Dunne . . . of the 99th Regiment presents his compliments to Sir Charles Phipps and begs to inform him that if the person in charge of Her Majesty's dogs will call at 31 Duke Street, St James's, about twelve o'clock tomorrow, Capt. Dunne will give him charge of the little dog and also all the necessary directions about its treatment.

At the time of Lootie's arrival neither Queen Victoria nor Tzŭ-hsi were empresses but 'empresses-in-waiting' as one might call them. Queen Victoria was not proclaimed Empress of India until 1876 – not until then could she sign her letters 'Victoria R.I.', Regina et Imperatrix, which she immediately did in a New Year card to Disraeli.

Many stories say that Tzŭ-hsi, twenty years younger, was given the title of Empress after the birth of her son in 1856, but the Chinese were more cautious than that; she was merely raised to Concubine of the Second Rank and was known in the Court as the Concubine Yi. Concubine? Queen Victoria would have raised shocked eyebrows, but in China concubines were as legally married to their lords as any wife. Tzŭ-hsi was, in fact, created Empress at the same time as the Emperor's official wife, Niuhuru when, after his death, they became joint regents for Tsŭ-hsi's infant son.

From the moment Princess Victoria was conceived it was possible that she would succeed to the English throne. Her father, the Duke of Kent, never doubted it; 'Look carefully at her', he would say of his baby daughter, 'She will be queen.' But it is ironical that she owed her existence and her long impeccable reign to two disreputable facts: the dissoluteness of her royal uncles and her father's enormous debts.

When, in 1817, Princess Charlotte, only child of the Prince Regent, died in childbirth, Parliament became seriously worried about the succession. The Prince himself was too far gone in decadence and illness to have another child; it was imperative for the remaining dukes to marry and, as the ballad-writer Peter Pindar wrote in fun, the hunt was on:

> Yoicks! The R...l sport's begun
> I'faith but it is glorious fun
> For hot and hard each R...l pair
> are at it hunting for the Heir.

The Duke of Sussex refused; the Duke of Clarence, later William IV, obliged but, though he had had ten lusty illegitimate children, those by his gentle wife Queen Adelaide were stillborn or lived only a few months. Next in succession came the Duke of Kent and for him it was a horrid dilemma. During twenty-seven years he had lived cosily with his mistress Madame de Laurent; they loved one another but ambition and the debts prevailed. Madame de Laurent, who acted with great dignity, retired to a Paris convent and Edward, Duke of Kent, married the widowed Princess of Leiningen who, as she already had two beautiful children, was obviously fertile. He brought her to England 'just in time' – it seemed of paramount importance that the child be born in England – and, on 24 May 1819, she arrived, 'a little Princess, plump as a partridge', which Queen Victoria remained all her life.

She was not the only royal baby born that year; the Clarences had a daughter who would have preceded the small Victoria but she died at four months old; the Dukes of Cumberland and Cambridge who had also obligingly married, each had a son but they were younger brothers to the Duke of Kent and, as England had no salic law, 'Little Victory' as Carlyle called her, was the heir.

The Prince Regent detested the Duke of Kent but when the soldier-duke died a year after his daughter's birth, the Prince grudgingly allotted apartments for her and her mother in Kensington Palace where the little Princess spent her days in the strictest of English nursery fashions; it was essential for the nation to be shown that she was being brought up to principles very different from the rest of the royal family and to appear as 'the very picture of a happy unspoilt child'. 'Happy', though, is doubtful; outside playmates were discouraged and Princess Victoria was never with anyone, child or grown-up, without a third person, usually her German governess, Baroness Lehzen, present. She slept in her mother's bedroom, was not even allowed to go up or downstairs without someone holding her hand. Even if she were unspoilt no one in the Household forgot for one moment her royal importance – a complete contrast to the childhood of Tzŭ-hsi, but then she was only the child of an insignificant government official.

> A little girl with almond-shaped eyes and her hair in two plaits down her back; small for her age, but quick-witted and quick-tempered; full of curiosity and determined not to miss anything that might be going on in the house or down the street – such a child must the little Chao have been, when she dwelt in Pewter Lane.
> . . . Chinese children are attractive little people, with impassive faces and sparkling black eyes . . . . The children in Pewter Lane must have learnt a lot about the ways of men, in their own courtyards and in the immediate neighbourhood. The Forbidden City was close by, a few hundred yards beyond the Jade Canal. One could see the yellow-tiled roofs gleaming in the sunlight and the hawks hovering round the towered Gate of Western Flowering. Behind those walls was the source of all power, of all riches, of all honour. Men called him the Son of Heaven.

It is a picturesque description of any little girl in Peking; her name though was not Chao, but Lan Kuei – Little Orchid – nor does it seem likely that Tzŭ-hsi came to live at Pewter Lane until her early teens; she spent her childhood in Anwei; all her life she remembered and loved the south, its rice-fields, great rivers, plains and sun and hated the fierce cold of the Peking winters, but no matter at what age she arrived at her

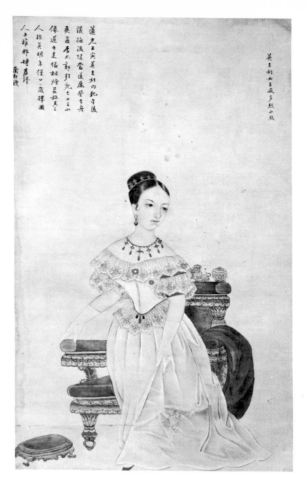

Portrait of Queen Victoria as a young girl, by a Chinese artist. The caption reads 'In 1842, Britain invaded up to Nanking. After reaching a negotiated settlement, I accompanied Chinese authorities and boarded British ships many times. British Chief showed us a picture of the Queen. Therefore I give this as a present. He also said that the Queen was very talented and shrewd and was only twenty-one years old. A gentleman with the name YA NA BO has been selected as her husband'

uncle's house, even she would not have dreamed she would one day rule that Son of Heaven.

Queen Victoria was made aware of her destiny in the famous description of the history lesson with Lehzen:

> On March 11th, 1830, after Mr Davys [her tutor] had gone home, Princess Victoria opened *Hewlett's Tables* of the Kings and Queens of England, to begin her history lesson with Lehzen. She found to her surprise that an extra page had been slipped into the book. 'I never saw that before', she exclaimed. 'No, Princess', said Lehzen. 'It was not thought necessary that you should.' Victoria studied the genealogical table . . . until she came to the names of her two uncles, George and William, and then her own. She drew the deduction. 'I am nearer the throne than I thought.' Then she burst into tears. After the 'little storm' had subsided . . . lifting up the forefinger of her right hand she spoke the famous words: 'I will be good'.

Victoria was sixteen years older than Tzŭ-hsi, becoming Queen when she was eighteen, the only surprise being that she succeeded so young. For Tzŭ-hsi at the same age, it was not only unlikely she would rule, but, as any statesman would have told her, impossible and, if the little English Queen could have known the way in which her fellow Empress, the only other woman who was to be her equal in the world, originally entered the palace of the Emperor, it would have seemed as fabled as King Solomon and his eight hundred wives or any Arabian Nights Tale, and that it happened as part of the pattern of a royal court of her own time, in a country with which her own was busily trading, unbelievably shocking.

In the Forbidden City or Imperial Palace of Peking more than six thousand humans lived and, among them all, only one whole man, the Emperor; every other male was an eunuch. Even the highest officials or visitors, even princes, were only allowed as far as the carefully guarded audience chamber; this to ensure the purity of the imperial line. For the Ch'ing or Manchu dynasty there was perhaps some reason for this: the Manchus were originally an independent, tough and warrior people and were not as effete or interbred as the Chinese aristocracy, among whom physical blemishes were frequent: goitres, squints, teeth grown together into one bone, deformed limbs, whilst almost all were marked by smallpox called, to palliate its horrid pitting, Celestial Flowers. To provide personnel for the palace young males were sold by their families or came from their own ambition, to be castrated. The dreadful operation was done in a special building near the imperial city gates: for three days the victim could not drink, but if he passed water on the third day he was likely to live; the wound took three months to heal.

Although some were quite active, eunuchs could never walk, much less run properly again but had the shuffle and tiny steps that, in the old days, Westerners came to associate with the Chinese. They lost their colour, were pale-skinned and usually gross, often not only in body but in appetite and took delight in titillating to excess any young or weak Emperor. Above all, they were in a position of immense power; everything in the palace went through their hands and they alone had private access to the Emperor and Empress. Of the three thousand or so women in the palace almost all were servants or maids-in-waiting but on the death of an Emperor, when the accustomed two years of mourning had passed, the mother of the heir and successor, chose for him twenty to thirty concubines and,

Summer Palace
one quarter scale

23 24
25

← 10 km NW

1 South Gate
2 Temple of Heaven
3 Temple of Agriculture
4 Chien Men gate
5 Tien An Men gate
6 Wu Men gate
7 Purple Forbidden City
8 Prospect Hill
9 White Dagoba
10 Pewter Lane
   Legation Quarter
   •••• start of siege
   ---- end of siege
11 British Legation
12 Russian   "
13 American   "
14 Japanese   "
15 French   "
16 German   "
17 Italian   "
18 Austro-Hungarian "
19 Customs Building
20 Hanlin Yuan
21 Tsungli Yamen
22 Northern Cathedral
23 Yuan Ming Yuan
24 European Palaces
25 I Ho Yuan
26 Kun Ming Lake
27 Jade Fountain Park

TARTAR CITY

IMPERIAL CITY

CHINESE CITY

0   1   2 km

Imperial Peking

Tzŭ-hsi as a young girl, the Concubine Yi

from among these, his official wife. The house law of the Ch'ing dynasty laid down that these concubines must be girls of one of the eight Banner classes, the hereditary Manchu warriors. When Tzŭ-hsi and her sister were fifteen and sixteen, the yellow palace carts – yellow was the Imperial colour – carrying couriers and preceded by heralds, rather as in the tale of Cinderella, came up Pewter Lane to summon the two girls for inspection; the new young Emperor, Hsien-fêng's, consort and concubines were being chosen.

Manchu dress was the same for men and women, a loose robe, gauze in summer, fur-lined in winter, worn over a tunic and pantaloons; for the rich the robe was embroidered with fantasies of flowers, dragons, lions, in gold thread studded with pearls and semi-precious stones. A woman's shoes, embroidered too, were like a soft clog on a high central sole five or six inches high; her hair was gathered up into a huge stiff decoration of jewels, ornamented stickpins, fanning out on either side and hung down with silk tassels and strings of pearls.

It made the neck look delicate and slim and echoed the almond shape of the eyes. 'A Manchu girl in full dress looked like a spring tree bowed with blossom', but however highly born, on coming to court she had to submit to an humiliating ordeal. The Chinese, like most orientals, dislike touch – except, of course, when making love. Chinese mothers do not kiss their babies, they delicately smell their necks and cheeks; no doctor was allowed to examine or touch a royal patient, yet these girls had to bear the lewd fingerings of the Chief Eunuch.

Tzŭ-hsi's sister was rejected and she herself appointed only as a Kuei Jen, concubine of the fifth and lowest rank, but the Imperial Emblem of the Manchu or Ch'ing Dynasty was a fitting symbol for this strange and ambitious girl – a Five-Clawed Dragon struggling to seize the Flaming Pearl of knowledge and power.

Even as a concubine she was still far from the Emperor; some of the chosen girls in the Palace never saw him, willy-nilly remaining virgin all their lives, and Tzŭ-hsi's family had no money to buy access through the Chief Eunuch, which was the usual way. She had nothing but her wits, which were considerable, and, though she had to wait three years for her chance, she did not waste them. It was unusual in the China of those days for girls to be educated – her own mother had opposed the small Orchid's learning to read – but Tzŭ-hsi found eunuch scholars to teach her at least a smattering of the classics and arts, poetry, singing, calligraphy and painting for which she had real talent, studies that, with her own natural eye and discernment, were to astound her contemporaries. Above all, she was interestingly different and amusing, as the young Emperor was to find: a 'golden-orchid friend' in Chinese idiom means one's especial soulmate; perhaps Hsien-fêng thought that in his 'Orchid' he had found her.

The story goes that, one afternoon, he walked, as he loved to do, in the gardens of the Summer Palace – the whole court moved there in the hot months of May, June, July – and, in a deep recess among the plane trees, he heard a girl singing; it was Tzŭ-hsi. Her song might have been one written by another concubine more than a thousand years before; she too came from the South and may well have known this solitary game of waiting for favour.

> . . . Sir, do not prize your coat of gold thread
> . . . Sir, prize the time of youth
> When the flower is ready for the plucking
> Straightaway it should be plucked.
> Do not delay until there is no flower
> and pluck an empty twig.

A Manchu lady and her dog

The Emperor stopped and asked whose voice it was.

Outside the imperial bed-chamber – to call it a bedroom seems inadequate – a table stood and, on it, was a jade tablet; there the Emperor wrote, or his mother hopefully wrote, the name of the concubine chosen for his bed that night. When the Chief Eunuch turned it over on the evening of that after-noon, the Emperor's own hand had written Tzŭ-hsi's name.

In England it was Queen Victoria who had the choice, but a strictly limited choice. From babyhood Prince Albert had been told that one day he would marry the English mayflower – Queen Victoria, as a girl, had a rosebud prettiness – 'a sonsy lass', said Carlyle. Albert was a long way down on the list of suitors but in the end, of course, it was he, Albert, 'who is beautiful', wrote the young Queen – she was always generous with her underlinings – 'Albert is really quite charming and so excessively handsome, my heart is quite going . . .' Soon it had quite gone! 'Oh to know I . . . am loved by such an angel . . . Oh, how I adore him,' – a feeling far removed from any felt by Tzŭ-hsi for Hsien-fêng. No two wedding nights could have been more different.

For the ceremony in Westminster Abbey Queen Victoria wore a white satin dress with English Honiton lace, a diamond necklace and Prince Albert's present of a sapphire brooch and a wreath of orange blossom; her twelve young train-bearers were in white, with white roses; all was innocence, sweetness – and restraint. After the wedding breakfast the pair drove to Windsor Castle. 'We had our dinner in our sitting room but I had such a sick headache I was obliged to lie down on the sofa but ill, or not ill, I never, never spent such an evening!!! My dearest, dearest sat on a footstool by my side. We kissed each other again and again.'

When the Chief Eunuch found Tzŭ-hsi's name on the jade

tablet, she was undressed, bathed and perfumed, then wrapped in a red quilt, carried naked to the Emperor's room and laid on the end of the imperial bed. It is told she took her small pekingese with her 'to give her courage' — that would not have been impossible; the little creature would certainly not have been afraid of the Emperor nor, as it was an imperial dog, would he have objected.

Etiquette laid down that the concubine should crawl up the bed to the Emperor's side but one cannot imagine Tzŭ-hsi crawling. The Son of Heaven was sickly, jaded with dissipation and indulgence — he often escaped from the tyranny of his court and bribed his eunuchs to take him to the bawdy tea-houses and opium dens of the Chinese city where the, to him, forbidden 'lily-footed' Chinese women could be found. He was sated with pornography, with books describing even more positions of love than the Hindu Kama Sutra, hundreds of attitudes with picturesque names: 'the Fish, Eye-to-Eye,' lying alongside each other; 'the White Tiger leaps', the woman taken from behind; 'Approaching the Fragrant Bamboo', both standing . . . and countless others. Tzŭ-hsi, in spite of all the stories told about her and her handsome soldier cousin, Jung-lu, was virgin, unlikely to have heard of any such wiles, yet, night after night, when the jade tablet was turned over, her name was there, and on 29 April 1856, in the Summer Palace, she gave birth to a son, Tsai-ch'un.

Terrible tales and legends have been woven around this baby; one that Tzŭ-hsi, after pretending pregnancy, smuggled him in then, allowing his real mother to visit him, had her strangled, but in a palace of several thousand jealous spies, this could not have been true. Some say the Emperor was sterile but he already had a daughter and later, by another concubine, a second son who died as a baby. There is no doubt that

Tzǔ-hsi's only child was also the Emperor's.

By that time Queen Victoria had borne eight of her nine children. Her marriage to Prince Albert was as idyllic as a royal marriage could be but, on her side, marred by the constant procession of babies. Though she loved children she had never liked, nor was ever to like, little babies . . . they were 'frog-like', 'ugly', and, even years later after the birth of a fourth child to the Prince and Princess of Wales, she was to write, 'A mere little red lump was all I saw, and I fear a . . . fourteenth grandchild becomes a very uninteresting thing . . . for it seems to me to go on and on like the rabbits in Windsor Park.'

She came to love her children, particularly as they grew older, but it was Albert, the Prince Consort, who really concerned himself with their nursery years – odd in those days of the lordliness of men – just as he took all the domestic side of the palaces into his hands, justifiably, as they were as abominably run as they were extravagant.

Windsor Castle

Most people have read of Prince Albert's economies with, for instance, the candles. He found that fresh ones were put into each room every day and yesterday's removed, even if they had not been lit. They were the perquisites of the servants, a little thing but it ran through every aspect of palace life. With German thoroughness he cleaned it all out and his principles remained long after him, though such minutiae often caused umbrage and trouble. There is on record an anguished letter from Mrs Henderson, housekeeper at Windsor in the eighties, to the Comptroller of the Lord Chamberlain's Department, about dusters:

> With reference to the 24 dozen of dusters reported as missing in our last quarterly return, I beg to remark that altogether there are between three and four hundred dozen in constant use, scattered all over the castle in the workshops, stores and outbuildings and that at my stock taking it is quite impossible to collect them all together, and although missing at the time, many may, and do, subsequently turn up. They are used for all sorts of hard work and rough purposes, and a very great many get worn out and thrown aside without our knowledge.

This parsimony extended even to the little Chinese dog's food.

> It is very dainty about its food [young Captain Hart Dunne had written], and won't generally take bread and milk, but it _will_ take boiled rice with a little chopped chicken and gravy mixed up in it and this is considered the best food for it.

Copy:

Buckingham Palace.
12 April 1861.

Dear Sir.

The bearer of this is the person who has charge of the Queen's dogs, & who would receive "Lootie." I think it right however to tell you, in consequence of your letter of last evening, that I am not authorized to hold out the expectation that this little dog will be received as a pet into the Queen's room. It will certainly not be put into the Kennel where the other dogs are kept, but will always live in a room. but H.M: has already a dog which remains in Her room, & it will depend upon the Queen's direction

---

A letter in which Sir Charles Phipps tells Captain Hart Dunne that
Lootie can expect no special privileges at Windsor

The kennelman forwarded this letter for Sir Charles Phipps's consideration as it was 'on a higher scale than he was accustomed to'. The answer came back:

> With regard to the little Chinese dog, I am desired to say [by Sir Charles] that he [sic] is to be treated with all possible kindness and fed upon nice cooked meat with breadcrumbs and powdered biscuit . . . after a little fasting and coaxing he will probably come to like the food that is good for him . . .

but left to himself Sir Charles was not so mild. On the outside of one of Captain Hart Dunne's letters he has written in pencil (or it may be by a later hand as the abbreviation seems strange so early), 'A Chinese dog, i.e. a peke, that insists on chicken in its dietary!' Evidently the kennel had had a struggle with Lootie! Sir Charles might have reflected that rice – and chicken – were commonplace in China, while beef, the cheaper cuts and entrails which were probably English kennel food, was taboo. He showed a lack of imagination and, considering the minute quantity of chicken or meat a small pekingese eats, perhaps three ounces a day, one feels that the Court might have risen to the expense.

The Empress Tzŭ-hsi would never have stinted anything in any way; with her astuteness, she must have been well aware that a great deal of the expense charged to the Privy Purse went on 'squeeze' or 'tea-money', but she also knew that, in the Orient at least, it was such an established custom that it was better to accept it; besides, the Chinese believed in magnificence. Under the Ch'ings the costs of the Court rose to the equivalent of 65,000,000 pounds sterling a year.

It was magnificent down to the least detail; an Imperial dog

An Imperial dog cage in cloisonné and white jade, 1736–95

cage, used for carrying the dogs between the different palaces, was of cloisonné and white jade; it had rings for carrying-poles, presumably borne by eunuchs . . . its cushion was of brocaded silk.

Fantastic 'embroideries' have grown up around the palace pekingese of this time: how, for instance, the puppies were suckled by palace women – which is most unlikely as even their milk teeth are sharp and human milk is so different from dog milk that they would not have thrived: how each had its attendant handmaid – in fact they were looked after by eunuchs who vied with each other to breed better and better specimens to please and impress their royal masters and mistresses.

It is true too that none of those dogs was allowed outside. A palace bird might be taken for an airing; a scarlet-throated thrush or a singing linnet carried on its perch, but the penalty for smuggling a pekingese out was death. How then did Lootie, who might have ridden in that exquisite cage, come to be sleeping in a soldier's forage cap?

'The Way of Heaven is fairness to all. It does not suffer us to harm others in order to benefit ourselves'. Long before Lootie's day, in fact in 1839, Lin Tsê-hsü, High Commissioner of Canton, had written these lines to young Queen Victoria. 'The English', he had reported to Peking, 'are ruled at present by a young girl, but I am told it is she who issues commands and on the whole it seems that it would be best to send instructions to her'. Send instructions. Poor Lin! The letter went on:

> Your country lies twenty thousand leagues away; but for all that the Way of Heaven holds good for you as for us, and your instincts are not different from ours; for nowhere are there men so blind as not to distinguish

between what brings life and what brings death, between what brings profit and what does harm. . . . Rhubarb, tea, silk are all valuable products of ours, without which foreigners could not live. The Heavenly Court, extending its benevolence to all alike, allow these things to be sold and carried away across the sea, not grudging them even to remote domains, its bounty matching the bounty of Heaven and Earth.

But there is a class of evil foreigner . . . tempting fools to destroy themselves, merely in order to reap profit. Formerly the number . . . was small, but now the vice has spread far and wide and the poison penetrated deeper and deeper . . . it appears that this poisonous article is manufactured by certain devilish persons in places subject to your rule . . . but careless of the lives of other people, indifferent in . . . greed for gain to the harm done to others; such conduct is repugnant to human feeling and at variance with the Way of Heaven . . . Do not say you have not been warned in time . . .

It was a wise good letter but it never reached Queen Victoria; if it had, Lord Palmerston would perhaps have been able to explain it away: trade was necessary. Trade was trade. 'But what', the Queen might have asked, 'was this dreadful poison?'

She would have been startled to know it came from a flower and that this flower was about to cause a war.

CHAPTER THREE

The Flower that made a War

The flower was a poppy – *papaver somniferum*: pink, purple, deep red or white, the colour made no difference.

For thirty centuries there had been trade between China and Europe; in return for the silks of Han, the Romans had sent weapons to China, and silver, horses – and dogs; the tradition of a Maltese strain in the breeding of the palace pekingese probably dated from this. The Silk Route, as it was called, lay through perilous country after it left the more populous way of the Spice Caravan Route from Turkey and Arabia, so that China itself was almost unknown, as was the rest of the world to China; but there were stories, brought by travellers, missionaries and, particularly, Mahommedan merchants, that told of a legendary land that lay far to the north of India; it was, said the stories, intensely civilised and called Cathay. These stories grew in credence, especially after the Jesuits, including that 'Wise Man from the West,' Father Matteo Ricci, had been allowed to establish themselves at Peking; he and his monks charmed the Emperor, Wan-li of the Ming dynasty, not by their religion but with their clocks and fountains, even building for him in the first Summer Palace a pseudo-temple unflatteringly known as the Barbarians' Castle.

> It must have been a monstrosity among perfection. For instance, . . . the Hall of the Peaceful Seas, with its horseshoe stairways, had fifty jets of water spurting from the balustrades. The space between the mounting steps was filled by an enormous shell. Below, sitting solemnly upright in a circle, were twelve bronze animals garbed in the robes of Buddhist monks.
> These animals, spouting water in turn, marked the hours, each beast presiding over a hundred and twenty consecutive minutes. In noting time the Chinese refer to the hour of the dog, the hour of the sheep, the hour of the rat. . . .

As the seventeenth century dawned a young Portuguese lay brother, Bento de Goes, who spoke fluent Persian, was given the task of attempting to find this Cathay. Disguised as a merchant he left Agra in 1602 and, three years later, having travelled through Kabul, Kashgar, Yarkand, the vast plateau and gorges of what is now Tibet, and across the dreaded Gobi desert, he succeeded in reaching the Great Wall of China and Suchow, where he died of his hardships, but was first able to despatch a letter to his superiors in Peking in which he established unmistakably that Cathay and China were the same.

The merchants brought back to China, among other things,

> vines, though the Chinese did not use them for their wine which was traditionally made from rice or wheat. The caravans also brought the pomegranate which, with its seeds, was to become the symbol of fertility. China,

The opium poppy

in its turn, sent cinnamon and flowers – many that seem natural to us were originally Chinese: syringa, narcissus, crab-apple, magnolias. The peach too, made its slow progress from China to England,

but the caravan routes grew more and more perilous and soon a sea passage was found – the Portuguese being the first sea-traders. China trustfully opened her ports and allowed a Portuguese settlement in a small island which became Macao; It was a foothold and these 'barbarian' traders were quickly followed by the Spanish, then the Dutch. The Chinese offered silk, porcelain, tea and the rhubarb Lin wrote of, which was deemed a necessity, especially in Victorian times; by the early seventeenth century England, nation of shopkeepers, had come upon the scene.

There is, in existence, a document* telling that during the great Thames Fair in Westminster Hall, held for the marriage of the Winter Queen, Elizabeth, sister of Charles I, to the Elector Palatine in 1613, a magnificent Chinese junk came sailing up the Thames. The crowds watching from the banks saw spits turning on the deck and, to their horror, saw too the carcases of dogs roasting on them. The junk was moored at Westminster Steps and a mandarin or grand official, perhaps even a prince, came up on deck and, when he had walked in his wonderful robes up the Steps at the entrance to the Hall with his train unfolded behind him, he bent down so that his wide sleeves touched the ground and there appeared from these what the crowd took to be gigantic butterflies, but they were pekingese of the then-called 'sleeve' size and these tiny dogs caught his train in their mouths and were his trainbearers.

* I wish I could find the document; it was seen and read by a lady on whose truth I can rely but who unfortunately did not note the source. There are, however, accounts in China of pekingese acting as royal train bearers and even today they like to pick up edges of cloth in their mouths. If the story is true these must have been the first pekingese to set foot in England.

It is thought that the junk came from Amsterdam and may
have been built there – could a junk have been seaworthy
enough to have made the long journey round the Cape? But it
was undoubtedly true that after the austerities of Cromwell, in
the Restoration of Charles II, the craze for the luxuries of
chinoiserie – European adaptations of Chinese designs –
reached its height.

There had been a few genuinely Chinese importations: porcelain, paintings on silk or rice paper, a little jade and lacquer,
but now the Cathay of imagination took first place; there were
'Chinese' designed prints on chintz; porcelain factories had
'China designs'; there was skilful lacquer – japanning, as it was
called – and Chinese Chippendale or, as Thomas Chippendale
preferred to name it, 'Chippendale in the Chinese taste'.
Whole rooms became Cathay, like the famous Chinese room
at Claydon House in Buckinghamshire. In France, when
Louis XIV wanted to make a summer retreat for Madame de
Montespan, it was a little pleasure house called the Trianon de
Porcelain, but the faience tiles, made in Delft, did not stand up
to the weather. Watteau was deeply influenced, and influenced hundreds of others, setting the pattern for rococo
chinoiserie over all Europe. Boucher, too, made chinoiserie
tapestries which were copied in factories everywhere, and the
fashion invaded gardens: the first chinoiserie garden ornament
known in England was the House of Confucius at Kew, a
mixture of pagoda and pavilion built in 1747; it was followed
by William Chambers's famous tall pagoda of 1762.

The craze invaded writing. Charles Lamb brought it beautifully down to earth in his 'Dissertation upon Roast Pork'. He
was more right than he knew; the Chinese dote on pork; it was
the favourite meat of Tzŭ-hsi, especially the rind, chopped in
small pieces and fried until it was so crisp it deserved its name,
Tinkling Bells.

A fanciful collage of Kew Gardens with Chambers's pagoda in the background and the author's pekingese in the foreground

Hans Andersen too, writing of Chinoiserie, conveyed the truth — or a little of the truth:

> You know, of course, that in China the Emperor is a Chinese and all his subjects are Chinese too . . . the Emperor's palace was made entirely of delicate porcelain; it was all so precious and fragile that you had to be tremendously careful how you touched anything: the garden was full of the rarest flowers and the loveliest of these had little silver bells tied to them which tinkled so that no one should go by without noticing them.

That is the opening of the story of The Nightingale. It is, of course, a fairy story and the Emperor in 1837, when Andersen started writing his tales, was not Chinese but Manchu, and many of his subjects were Tartars and tribesmen, but in the famous paeony terraces of Loyang, during the T'ang dynasty, bells of silver were attached to the most precious blooms to frighten away birds or vibrate as footsteps passed them.

Chinoiserie was, of course, nonsense, often exquisite and always expensive as nonsense usually is; by the mid-nineteenth century it was on the wane. The satirists had long been pouring acid on the craze; in one of his plays Oliver Goldsmith had a Chinese appear before a lady of fashion:

> When the footman informed her grace that I was the gentleman from China, she instantly lifted herself from the couch, while her eyes sparkled with unusual vivacity. 'Bless me! . . . What an unusual share of somethingness in his whole appearance! Lord, how I am charmed with the outlandish cut of his face! . . . I would give the world to see him in his own country dress. Pray turn about, Sir, and let me see you behind.

. . . You that attend there, bring up a plate of beef cut into small pieces; I have a violent passion to see him eat. Pray, Sir, have you got your chop-sticks about you? . . . Pray speak a little Chinese.' Then she said in commendation, 'I have got twenty things from China that are of no use in the world. Look at those jars, they are of the right pea-green? . . .' 'Dear Madam,' said I, 'these, though they may appear fine to your eyes, are but paltry to a Chinese; but, as they are useful utensils, it is proper that they should have a place in every apartment.' '*Useful*! Sir,' replied the lady; 'sure you mistake, they are of no use in the world.' 'What! are they not filled with an infusion of tea as in China?' replied I . . . . 'I protest,' says the lady . . . .'

Chinoiserie did not appeal to Queen Victoria; she was appalled by her uncle, George IV's Pavilion at Brighton –'A strange odd-looking Chinese thing' – but trade was another matter. Trade, real exchange between countries, was vital, but it seemed that the Chinese, those, to Western ideas, 'topsy-turvey' people – even their books read back to front – did not wish to trade.

In 1715 the East India Company which had the monopoly of all Britain's trade with Asia and which was as powerful as it was persistent, had been allowed to establish a 'waterfront' of 'factories' or warehouses at Canton, to which goods were ferried back and forth from ships anchored out at sea. The Company had to observe the 'Eight Regulations' which forbade, amongst other things, any armed ships in the Pearl River on which Canton stood – all the Company's clippers were armed. The Eight Regulations forbade any contact, except through accredited dealers or 'hongs'; forbade any sedan-chairs, boating for pleasure excursions; more than a limited number of Chinese servants and, above all, any credit or smuggling, and it was repeated that the ships must anchor out to sea. These 'Regulations' Peking thought would make the 'barbarians' harmless; the British broke them all.

At first they tried diplomacy; in the reign of George III, Lord Macartney, handsome and skilled diplomat, was sent as England's first emissary to the Manchu Emperor, Ch'ien-lung, to try and persuade him to extend the British trade from the limitations of Canton to other ports and establish a British ambassador in Peking, in fact to make friendly relations between the two great Empires of the West and East. The mission was as costly as it was brilliant, and included magnificent presents; it was only as the houseboat sent to meet him sailed up the Pei-ho river to Peking that Lord Macartney realised that its flag bore an inscription: 'Tribute Embassy from the Red Barbarians'.

He was allowed to see the Emperor but not in the Forbidden City of innermost Peking; he was received informally in the Imperial Hunting Lodge at Jehol beyond the Great Wall and even then only in a pavilioned tent set up in the grounds.

The entry of an emperor is always impressive and never more so than with the Chinese; stories are told that, as the Imperial processions entered the Hall of Audience, specially trained palace pekingese carried the Emperor's train in their mouths as at the Thames Fair; there is no corroboration of this, but during the Sung dynasty, it is fact that the Emperor T'ai-tsung was always preceded into the Hall by that Peach Flower, already referred to, who barked to announce the Emperor's arrival.

In 1709 Peter the Great sent an embassy to Peking and the ambassador wrote of the Imperial dogs:

Everything was entered in a book, the names and qualities of each particular dog. There was also tied about its neck a yellow silk cord through a hole in a little bit of wood which hung from the dog's neck as a mark of its belonging to the court.

Evidently the Russian ambassador had been allowed to see the Imperial dogs which, though Ch'ien Lung undoubtedly had many, Lord Macartney was not – there is no mention of them in his description of the Emperor's entrance:

> The Imperial Cortège was heralded first by the sound of distant drums. The Everlasting Lord was seated in an open palanquin borne by sixteen eunuchs and preceded by others who called aloud his many styles: around them were umbrella men and musicians; he was dressed in plain dark silk, his silk boots embroidered with golden dragons and wore a velvet cap on which was a large pearl, his only ornament!

This was again the Flaming Pearl, mark of the Ch'ings; only the Emperor was allowed to wear it. His boots cost the equivalent of a hundred pounds in those days, and he never wore the same pair twice.

Lord Macartney was so impressed that, going down on one knee, he overbalanced and almost went down on both, bending over, so that unfortunately he gave the impression that he had made a partial kow-tow.

When any of the Emperors took his throne in the Hall of Audience, the suppliants, as they were called, had, at a herald's command, to kneel, touch the ground three times with their foreheads and, at a second command, rise; this ceremony was

Painting of dogs, showing pedigree neck-tags with tassels

repeated three times. The kow-tow had tremendous significance as it was an acknowledgement that the Emperor of China was the Son of Heaven, Lord of the Entire World.

Lord Macartney had suggested on meeting the Emperor he should observe the same ceremony as when meeting his own King: going down on one knee to kiss the royal hand. The Chinese were shocked as, for any human – except for necessary attendant eunuchs and chosen palace women – to touch the 'Sacred Person' was a capital offence. Had he been received in Peking, in the strict etiquette of the Hall of Audience in the Forbidden City, Lord Macartney would have had to make the kow-tow and when, in 1816, Lord Amherst followed him with another splendid British mission, this time to Ch'ien-lung's successor, the new embassy met a deadlock – no kow-tow, no Emperor; indeed, the Emperor wrote to the Prince Regent complaining of the ambassador's lack of politeness but, with Confucian gentleness, added, 'If you loyally accept our sovereignty there is really no need of these stated appearances' – of Macartneys and Amhersts – 'to prove that you are indeed OUR vassal'.

It seems extraordinary, with all the comings and goings of merchants and caravans, that the Chinese should not have heard of other Emperors, not even of the Moghuls of India or any of the great European dynasties; but up to the nineteenth century, Peking's scholars were still assuring the Emperor that England was a little island, a dependency of Holland or, sometimes, of Sweden, and that all nations, no matter how far away, were vassal states of China.

Deceived by the friendliness of Ch'ien-lung and the lavish hospitality, Lord Macartney had, for a while, been optimistic; he had not known the rule, handed down from the Han dynasty, that the three cardinal virtues of government are to

simulate affection, to express honeyed sentiments, to treat in-
feriors as equals – up to a point – and, one might add, 'to
grant precisely nothing'. If his mission was a failure, Lord
Amherst's was a fiasco and the English saw they would have to
trade from the restrictions of the Cantonese waterfront, as they
had done for the last hundred years, or else use force.

They chose force and, in 1839, there began one of the most
disgraceful wars ever fought in history; disgraceful because,
behind the English persistence and bullying, in which they
were soon joined by the French, was the real cause of the
Chinese rebuffs and alarms, terror of the insidious and
poisonous fruit of that poppy – opium.

In India and in the Middle and Far East, poppy fields were
planted in autumn, gathered in spring; just before the petals
fell the pods were gashed in the evening to let the 'white tears'
exude and be gathered at dawn next day. The juice was
simmered over a low fire – charcoal in the old days – allowed
to dry and the crust removed. This was repeated six times,
then the pure opium was smeared on wooden boards and left
to be dried in the sun.

Opium was known to every ancient civilisation, among them
the Assyrian, Greek and Indian. It was the aspirin of Europe:
doctors prescribed it for George IV; it had sometimes start-
lingly beautiful results – Coleridge wrote 'Kubla Khan' under
its influence. Berlioz ate some, vomited violently, emerged
purged, as it were, and found the inspiration for his Sym-
phonie Fantastique. The virtuous William Wilberforce took
it every day; it was given to babies, as it is in India even now.
Though it contained, among other things, morphine, from
which heroin is made, no one thought of it as harmful until
the English began trading with it in China.

The East India Company had planted fields of opium in

The Falcon

Bengal so that the valuable crop lay close at hand. Chinese goods used to be paid for in silver but, after 1800 at least, England was short of bullion – then how much easier to pay in opium. True, it was forbidden, its import breaking the Eight Regulations, but it was too lucrative to resist and floating island warehouses began to be anchored off Canton; cases of opium were smuggled from them in small boats to creeks and shallow harbours; a small army of unofficial 'hongs' sprang up and, like the official 'hongs', grew immensely rich – as did the British; there are many many illustrious families in England who owe their fortunes to opium.

The great tea-clippers of the China Run, with their yearly 'race' home to England or America are known to everybody, yet few people have heard of the opium fleet. One company alone, Jardine and Matheson, had a dozen or more clippers, heavily armed and magnificently equipped. Their flagship was the *Falcon*.

> She was a full-rigged ship, massively but beautifully masted in rake and proportions. Her yards and spars were equal to those on a ship of twice her capacity. It was her breadth of beam that enabled her to carry such a spread. Her fittings were unusually elegant, substan-

tial and costly. Where metal was employed it was mostly brass and copper, and this included even the belaying pins. The stanchions, sky-lights and coamings were of mahogany. The officers' cabins were extravagantly luxurious. . . . She was fast, yet dry, lively yet stiff. . . . Nothing in still life could be more picturesque than her sails which, unfurled at anchor or in a calm, fell in full heavy graceful folds from her yards and booms. Nothing could confer so strikingly the same triumph of art, when the same sails were filled and trimmed . . . . 'She can do everything but speak,' was a common remark among the crew.

To the average Englishman, poison was certainly too strong a word for opium, but then in Europe the drug was carefully prescribed. The Indian variety was also stronger than other kinds and it devastated the Chinese people, from the Emperor himself to the coolie who would spend his pitiful string of cash (Chinese coins were carried threaded on a string) for a few whiffs of opium instead of on food for his starving family. Its effects began to be known – hallucinations, ecstatic dreams, succeeded by an inertia from which the addict could not be roused and which left him in the useless apathy that Tennyson was to describe in *The Lotos-Eaters*:

Let us alone. Time driveth onward fast,
And in a little while our lips are dumb.
Let us alone. What is it that will last?
All things are taken from us, and become
Portions and parcels of the dreadful Past.
Let us alone. What pleasure can we have
To war with evil? Is there any peace
In ever climbing up the climbing wave?

All things have rest, and ripen toward the grave
In silence; ripen, fall and cease:
Give us long rest or death, dark death, or dreamful ease.

Lin Tsê-hsü was not the only official Chinese or Englishman
who protested. 'How stands our national character in the
East?' asked an English missionary in 1839. 'We are seen con-
tinually implicated in iniquities which the natives of India and
China have discernment enough to look at with detestation.'

Is it not the fact that at one time (and not more than a
century back) many ports along the coast of China . . .
were open to our commerce, which are now entirely
closed? So that *our restriction to the single port of Canton* is,
comparatively, *a recent thing; and may be considered as the
just and natural consequence of our own misdeeds.* The
heathen government of China has long regarded opium
smoking, and the opium trade with such just and
merited abhorrence, that it utterly refuses to grow rich
and to increase its resources, by the sanction of one or
the other! Shall *we*, then, consent, as Christians and as
Britons, to lend ourselves to this traffic?

Nobody listened and Lin Tsê-hsü's second letter to England
was frantic and, unfortunately, as ignorant as it was insulting:

You savages of the further Seas have waxed so bold, it
seems, as to defy and insult our mighty Empire. Of a
truth it is high time for you to 'flay the face and cleanse
the heart', and to amend your ways. If you submit
humbly to the Celestial dynasty and tender your
allegiance, it may give you a chance to purge yourselves
of your past sins. But if you persist and continue in

your path of obstinate delusion, your three islands [sic] will be laid waste and your people pounded into mincemeat, as soon as the armies of his Divine Majesty set foot upon your shores.

The mincemeat was on the other side. The British declared war in 1840 and, no match for their warships and guns, the Chinese were defeated and Lin had to make the Treaty of Nanking, by which four more ports were opened to the foreigners. Opium was not even mentioned – but the wars dragged on for more than twenty years.

Battle after battle was fought along the coasts, treaty after treaty made only to be broken by one side or the other. Peking was two thousand miles away, still partially blind to the danger and after Nanking, Lin was blamed for weakness, recalled and tried for treason. The Grand Secretary Kishen was sent in his place but quickly succumbed to the bribes of 'secret offers'; he too was recalled and more severely treated. When it was found that he owned 425,000 acres of land, 135,000 ounces of gold, a vast hoard of silver, eleven boxes of jewels, besides shares in ninety banks, he was executed. The 'hongs' grew uneasy as their least dealings with the 'barbarians' began to be scrutinised.

In 1843 one of them, a mandarin, came for help to a young English naval officer with whom he had made friends; the Englishman spoke Chinese, a rare accomplishment in those days, and had often dined with his friend. One evening, after greeting him as an honoured guest, the mandarin had drawn from the folds of his coat a little dog, saying it was his most precious possession.

The little animal slept on his couch beside him, and knew his thoughts and wishes . . . and had a marvellous

instinct as to the worth of human beings. The little
creature had aroused him many times when danger
threatened, and had saved him from fire only the pre-
vious night by jumping on him and awakening him, for
the brazier had in some way set light to the covering of
his couch. He [the mandarin] related many incidents
concerning the marvellous knowledge possessed by his
little dog, which was the size of his master's muff
(carried by all mandarins in winter) . . . . Now the
mandarin was in great danger . . .. That evening he gave
a huge 'joss' [or idol] to the young officer, begging him
to guard his most precious jewel and make use of the
fortune contained therein. The joss was as big as a large
child; the figure was in wood, lacquered red and gold;
and the large hole at the back of the image had a little
golden door or lattice. The ship was at the moment
sailing for England, and on perceiving a movement behind the latticework, it was opened, and there was the
little dog . . . lying on a cushion. During a long voyage
the little creature proved the most devoted companion
of the officer and was beloved by the crew, but it did
not live to reach England.

The friendship between the mandarin and young officer was
not surprising; the English and the Chinese of the old days had
many things in common, not only in their love of dogs and
birds; both had a wry humour, believed in understatement and
shared a passion for gardens and flowers; both relished
eccentricity and practised ancestor worship – the Chinese
openly, the English in private; yet throughout two Opium
Wars the British commanders behaved with such boorishness
and rudeness that it is difficult to believe that in their own

The English trade in opium; a French view. 'You're to buy this poison immediately so that we can have lots of tea to digest our roast beef'

country they were courteous well-bred men.

They had long needed a stick with which to strike the final blow that would, they said, bring China to her senses. In 1856 the British found it in the affair of the *Arrow*, a small Chinese boat chartered by the English and flying the Union Jack; on a journey from Canton to Hongkong, then in British hands, she was boarded by Chinese troops, her Chinese crew taken off and the flag pulled down. An apology was demanded which the new Governor of Canton refused and the incident was quickly magnified into an insult. For the French the provocation was the murder of a French missionary, said not only to have been killed but eaten. In 1857 the natives of Canton burned the British warehouses to the ground. On Christmas Day of that year Canton was recaptured by the British and Lord Elgin, son of the Elgin of the Marbles, as leader of the punishing force was instructed to demand more open ports and insist on the establishment of a British Residency or Embassy in Peking itself.

This was refused; the Chinese had seen what the English had done in India, 'encroaching . . . like silk-worms eating mulberry leaves' and, at last, the court in Peking grew frightened – though not frightened enough.

They still believed that the 'thousand thousand' Chinese forces could overcome the foreigners, but in 1858 the Taku forts which Peking had thought impregnable were taken and yet another treaty had to be signed, the Treaty of Tientsien, by which China had to concede still more ports and the import of opium, willy-nilly, was made legal. The treaty also laid down that foreigners were never again to be described as 'barbarians', and an ambassador from each country would live in one of the ports and visit Peking as he chose.

The treaty was signed but, a year later, the Chinese, who had rebuilt the Taku forts, saw not an embassy but eighteen English and French gunboats coming up the Pei-ho river that led to Peking. The Chinese impetuously opened fire, sinking four ships and killing eighty-nine men. Each side said the other had violated the treaty and finally Lord Elgin, in command of the English, and Baron le Gros of the French, offered to come to Peking with no more than a thousand troops bringing a letter to the Emperor from Queen Victoria. The offer was accepted and an advance party of English officers and men, with a few Sikh cavalry, was despatched to make arrangements. The troop carried a white flag but on the way back was ambushed, not on government orders, it was said, but by a Manchu war party. All of the captives were thrown into a criminals' prison, kept in filth and degradation without food and water and were tortured. Many of them died. This was unforgiveable treachery and full battle broke out; soon the British and French decided to advance on Peking.

On 6 September the Emperor issued a panic-stricken edict to his people, said to have been dictated by Tzŭ-hsi, in which he offered, 'For the head of a black barbarian [the Sikhs who were fighting for the English] 50 taels: for the head of a white barbarian, 100 taels', and went on, 'I command all my subjects, Chinese and Tartar, to hunt the Barbarians down like savage beasts. Let the villages be abandoned as these wretches draw near. Let all provisions be destroyed. In this manner, their accursed race will perish of hunger like fish in a dried-up pond.'

He appealed to deaf ears; not a month later Lord Elgin was informed that 'by law the Emperor was obliged to hunt in the autumn' which was a face-saving way of saying he and his Court had fled to Jehol in the north beyond the Great Wall. Peking lay at the enemies' mercy and, ten miles from the city, they discovered the Summer Palace, the Yuan-ming Yuan,* the largest, and perfection, of all Chinese gardens.

There had been a Summer Palace from the first centuries A.D., but this of the Yuan-ming Yuan had been begun in the

---

* This was the old Summer Palace. Tzŭ-hsi built a new one, using only one section of the old.

seventeenth century by the early Manchu emperors as a modest, almost picnic, retreat from the summer heat of Peking. Then Ch'ien-lung, the inimitable, came to the Dragon Throne and with his wealth and connoisseur's eye, he was able to create literally hundreds of gardens in the Yuan-ming Yuan.

If ever there were an Emperor I should have liked to have known it was Ch'ien-lung, grandfather-in-law to Tzŭ-hsi with whom, had he known her, he could have shared many of his delights: poetry, painting, calligraphy, gardens and flowers. He was a true poet and a scholar; the people said he must secretly have been born of Chinese parents and could not possibly be one of the philistine warrior tribe of Manchus; yet he was a warrior, indeed a conqueror, and showed all the Manchu firmness, ruling the Chinese empire for fifty-nine years from 1736 to 1795. He had, too, what few of the Chinese Emperors or Empresses seem to have had, a conscience – though he could forget to use it; he spent stupendously on the building of the original Summer Palace, tempted by its beauty. 'I admit my fault but can't avoid it', he wrote, and went on spending.

A palace built over a rivulet he called the Happy Place of Falling Streams. The magnolia grove, the Realm of Fragrance. The Garden of Aquatic Grasses had a secondary meaning implying that it was the Retreat for Graceful Literary Effort. A favourite spot was known as A Stream, Trees and a Bright Lute. The most resplendent of the gardens was the Peony Terrace, the Mou Tan Tai, where Ch'ien-lung admired the flaunting vermilion flowers and looked out across the gleaming Lake of the Nine Islands.

White paeony, 10th—11th century

There was the Imperial Hunting Park, the Jade Fountain Park, the palaces built by the Jesuits and the Garden of Clear Rippling Waters, set a little away.

In naming his gardens the Emperor took special pride. He searched for the appropriate title, then with firm brush-strokes drew the ideographs on tautly stretched silk. Finally the inscription was cut in stone.

Ch'ien-lung composing verses in his garden

The name he gave to the Yuan-ming Yuan is a subtle one; translated literally it means the Round Bright Garden but this was not because it was round, nor bright; the Chinese ideograph for 'round' suggests the complete, the perfect, the ideal of a good man, while that for 'bright' suggests the power of such a man to illuminate the lives of others, so that the Round Bright Garden, or Mirror Garden as it was sometimes called, reflected the ideal of a pure soul.

It was to last less than a hundred years.

The French were there first. On 6 October they found the palaces deserted except for a few terrified eunuchs. The English followed next day but by then the French had taken almost everything. The looting and destruction is best told by the officers and men who took part:

> Imagine three thousand men after a hard campaign suddenly let loose into a city of priceless museums . . . officers and men seemed to have been seized with a temporary insanity in body and soul. They were absorbed in one pursuit, which was plunder, plunder, plunder . . . . Often the men, in a soldier's ridiculous way, dressed themselves in the richly-embroidered gowns of the women, and almost all had substituted the turned-up Mandarin hat for their ordinary forage cap.

> I saw a troop of Sikh cavalry, their appearance was ludicrous for each sowar had about twenty-four rolls of silk piled up before and behind his saddle so that he could hardly get his hands over to hold the reins.

> We came upon a summer-house with ten or twenty rooms in it – sleeping rooms and sitting rooms – all filled, furnished, and ready for the immediate reception

of a nobleman. The furniture of this one summer-house would sell at home for a prince's ransom. In the cupboards of the wall were boxes of the Imperial yellow china, each cup being wrapped in soft paper and in its own wooden compartment, being deemed as precious. Some of the finest 'cracle' was so minute that you must get a good light to see it in. Some had the five-clawed dragon finely worked in it – invisible when you looked directly at it.

For knick-knacks and bijoux the French camp offered the greatest allurement . . . . You had only to ask the first French soldier you met if he had anything for sale and he would produce gold watches, strings of jewels, jade ornaments . . . .

The British share of the plunder was all arranged for exhibition in the hall of the large temple where the headquarters staff were quartered, and a goodly display it was. White and green jade-stone ornaments of all tints, enamel-inlaid chairs . . . bronzes, gold and silver figures, statuettes, etc., fine collections of furs, many of which were of much value . . . sable, sea-otter, ermine, Astrakhan lamb, etc., and court costumes among which were two or three of the Emperor's state robes of rich yellow silk, worked upon with dragons in gold through-out, and beautifully woven with floss silk embroidery on the skirts, the inside being lined with silver fur and ermine, and cuffed with glossy sable.

At the end of the hall were piled immense quantities of rolls of silk and crape of various colours, several of the beautiful imperial yellow, the kind prescribed for the use of His Imperial Majesty alone.

A small yellow teacup realised £22, [probably now £20,000] there was a necklace of green jade with rubies, a beautiful gold jug from which the Emperor of China used to pour rosewater over his delicate hands.

The soldiers also came across two presents made by Lord Macartney to the Emperor Ch'ien-lung, a stagecoach and two twelve-pound howitzers, carefully preserved. Why they were never used against the French and English is a mystery.

Then, on 18 October, Lord Elgin ordered the Summer Palace to be burnt. 'It took two days: during them the light was so subdued by the over-hanging clouds of smoke that it seemed as if the sun itself was undergoing an eclipse' – fittingly so, the disgraced Emperor was the Lord of Heaven. 'The world around looked dark with shadow.'

It is said that Lord Elgin was haunted by the burning for the rest of his life. At the time he believed he was justified; he had pledged himself not to destroy Peking but the firing on his ships without warning in the Pei-ho river and the treatment and deaths of the English and Indian prisoners taken in the ambush had to be avenged. Reparation in fines of money would have meant taxes on the Chinese people who were not to blame, punishment for the culprits would have ended in some probably innocent officials being sent to the British and French for execution which, in any case, was an everyday event in China. The loss of his palace was a blow that fell directly on the Emperor, inflicting, to an oriental, the worst punishment of all, loss of face.

They came to the secluded summer palace to
    escape the heat;
But now the east wind sweeps the royal road

> And grass grows rankly year by year;
> In the setting sun it's cold under
> The pines; no-one's about;
> Will-o'-the wisps play high, play low, shine brightly,
>   disappear.
> What nights of song, of dance and feasting!
> Hair in the mirror shows
> A stealthy change from dark to grey.
> In hearts of men an endless sorrow flows.

That was written in the time of the Six Dynasties, more than a thousand years before; it seems the Summer Palace was destined to be destroyed – this was the third time. The British wished to inflict an enduring hurt on the Chinese. They did far more – they deprived the world.

Hsien-fêng died soon after without returning to Peking.

Prince Kung, entrusted with the Emperor's Great Seal so that he was entitled to make terms with the enemy, was the first Chinese to understand something of the foreigner and the world beyond China. Though, in 1860, he was only twenty-seven, a little light man, so shortsighted he appeared to squint, he was a great statesman and was to serve his country and the Empress Tzŭ-hsi selflessly for the next twenty-three years only to be rewarded by being banished. His private seal had the inscription 'no private heart' – which was just as well. On 24 October, Lord Elgin met him at Peking. Colonel Wolseley of the Wiltshire Regiment described it:

> His Lordship travelled in a sedan chair of large pro-
> portions, painted red and hung about with streaming
> tassels of many colours in the approved Chinese
> fashion. Eight Chinese coolies in gorgeous scarlet

The entry of Lord Elgin into Peking on 24 October 1860

clothing carried the chair; a hundred cavalry and four hundred infantry escorted it with a numerous retinue of officers of all corps. The 2nd Division lined the route. It was a fine day, bright and warm, as they marched through the capital, colours flying, bands playing.

Prince Kung advanced to meet them making a stiff bow and shaking his own hands vigorously after the ordinary manner of Chinese etiquette, and the final treaty was signed.

It must have been a bitter moment. Prince Kung had to concede everything the Chinese had fought to keep inviolate; the ports were to be open to trade, the import of opium still to be legal; embassies of the Western nations were to have permanent residence in Peking and their representatives to be received by the emperor – without the kow-tow.

Yet China, if not Cathay, was still fabulous. The list of articles in the Tariff of Imports begins:

elephants' teeth, whole
elephants' teeth, broken
feathers, kingfisher and peacock

and includes gold thread, real or imitation: gum dragon's blood: mother-of-pearl: musical boxes: opium: dried prawns: rose maloes: sandalwood: sea-horse's teeth: shark fins: tiger bones: fragrant woods: corals, real or false: false pearls – real pearls were perhaps still imperial. There were also joss-sticks, paper umbrellas, musk, dried lily flowers, lichees – and, though not listed and only little by little, a flow of pekingese.

During the looting of the Summer Palace, three young officers came upon a pavilion, apparently deserted but with a shuttered room that was locked. Frantic barking came from inside and, on bursting open the door, they found the body of a Court lady guarded by five tiny dogs. She was a princess, or the Emperor's aunt, or a maid-of-honour, they could not tell which, but it was obvious that she had committed suicide rather than fall into enemy hands. The young officers took the five dogs and brought them to England.

That story appears in almost every book written about pekingese and is most picturesque, but unfortunately there is no mention of it in any letters or diaries written by anyone who took part in the looting and, of the three officers who supposedly broke down the door, Lord John Hay was in command of the frigate *Odin*, Sir George Fitzroy was also a naval officer, and all warships had orders to stay out in the river guarding the entrance to Peking, while Captain Hart Dunne, as he himself wrote, bought Lootie in the French camp. What is true is that the first pekingese dogs to appear in England came from the Summer Palace, were perhaps bought in the French camp or later from the few eunuchs left behind. Lord John brought home two pekingese though not, it seems, until 1863, as he stayed in the Eastern Command for another two years. Sir George Fitzroy also brought a pair, the fifth was Lootie, and there were more. As Captain Hart Dunne's letters affirm, Lord

Elgin had 'one', though it died on the long voyage home; some may have been bought by less exalted soldiers — in 1861 a Captain Wingfield showed at a Birmingham Show what was called 'A sacred Chinese dog, Joss . . . .'.

They were listed in France in the book *Histoire physiologique et anecdotique des chiens de toutes les races* by Bénédict Henri Revoil, published in 1867, where pekingese are described as 'chiens Chinois ramenés du Palais de Yung-Ming Yeng,' meaning the Yuan-ming Yuan, but it seems they too were brought back by ordinary soldiers, not even officers, as, for a long time, in France they were regarded as common little dogs — chiens des concierges — and did not regain their aristocracy until the Pekingese Club of Paris was founded.

A few of the wartime diaries do mention the palace dogs. One says so many were left behind they were 'taken away in cartloads and sold', but as, for the next forty years, pekingese remained extremely rare, even in Peking, this is obviously an exaggeration — unless the little dogs were eaten; they would have been a succulent dainty for the ordinary Chinese.

Another account tells that fourteen of the palace dogs 'were found drowned in a well to prevent them falling into barbarian hands', and this may be true; jumping down wells was a favoured way of Chinese suicide, especially among women — a fact which added to the problems of the French and English quartermasters in getting drinking water.

A Dr Rennie, writing in 1865, states that some of the dogs were taken forcibly from Chinese owners during the occupation of the city in 1861, which means some of the citizens of Peking may have stolen them. He himself bought one for two and a half dollars, perhaps the lowest price ever offered for a pekingese, but adds that 'the difficulty of obtaining them from the time when the Court returned [in 1861] up to the Boxer rebellion, together with the long voyage to Europe accounts for the fact that so few palace specimens were imported'.

The Book of Rites lays down that: 'in presenting the gift of a dog, it is to be led by the left hand, so that the right hand may restrain the dog from biting'. If Captain Hart Dunne had been able, as he obviously hoped, to present Lootie to Queen Victoria in person, would Lootie have dared to bite? The question did not arise because it is doubtful if the Queen ever saw her. There is a disappointed letter from the young Captain to Sir Charles Phipps:

> . . . I see by the papers that Her Majesty returns shortly to Osborne without going to Windsor.
> Will you pardon the suggestion that the little dog which you were kind enough to interest yourself about should be some day sent over to Richmond to be shown to the Queen.
> I would not have taken the liberty of mentioning this to you only that Colonel Crealock [?] tells me that the only other little animal of the same description which Lord Elgin was bringing home has lately died, and it would be a great pity after all its travels if 'Lootie' should do likewise before it is seen by Her Majesty.

We do not know if the Queen saw her or not. When she was accepted Captain Hart Dunne had written 'The only wish Capt. Dunne has about the dog is that it should be treated as a pet, not as a curiosity,' which was exactly what Lootie became. She was written about in the *Illustrated London News* which carried a poor drawing of her; she was written about in the *Ladies' Kennel Journal*, and the Queen had her painted by Keyl, a pupil of Landseer, but she lived out the rest of her life in the Home Park kennels. Sir Charles Phipps had written most reasonably from Buckingham Palace, 'I am not authorised to hold out the expectation that this little dog will be received as a pet into the Queen's room. Her Majesty already has a dog which remains in Her room'.

Captain Hart Dunne climbed down: 'I only hoped it would be made more or less a pet of by the Royal Family. I am perfectly contented to let its future claims to favouritism rest entirely on its own merits'. It is difficult to understand why he persisted; perhaps he hoped for notice, or promotion; or perhaps circumstances at home may have made it impossible for him to keep Lootie, but he even wrote to Copley, the head kennelman: 'If it is not made much of it will die'. Lootie must have been 'made much of' by someone, as she lived for another eleven years, but not with the Queen or any member of the Court.

Lootie's eyes, as they look out from her portrait, have a steady patience; her collar of bells has been taken off and lies in the foreground, but she is still a prisoner. In the background stands a porcelain vase painted with the exotic birds and flowers of her Chinese homeland but at her feet is that posy of English flowers, a pansy, a scarlet and a white geranium. On her forehead is that white mark of rank; Lootie has dignity but, as well as patience, there is sadness in those eyes.

'She belonged, I was told, to the Empress or a Court lady,' Captain Hart Dunne had written. It would hardly have been the Empress or Lootie would not have been left behind in the flight, but it might have been the unknown princess, or the Emperor's aunt, or a maid-of-honour. By the time this portrait was painted that 'someone' of the old Summer Palace was long dead, but dogs have long memories too. One of the oldest poems in the world is a poem of grief written by a Chinese:

> The sound of her silk skirt has stopped.
> On the marble pavement dust grows.
> Her empty room is cold and still.
> Fallen leaves are piled against her door
>   Longing for that lovely lady
> How can I bring my heart to rest?

Yet, if those five little dogs and perhaps a few companions had not been seized and brought to Britain and a few more had not followed them after the concessions forced on the Chinese, the breed might have become extinct.

It is not for nothing then that in Chinese calligraphy the word 'crisis' is made up of two characters: the first means 'danger', the second 'a turning point' or 'opportunity', perhaps it could be interpreted as hope.

CHAPTER FOUR

The Winter Castle and the Summer Palace

In November 1861 the Imperial Court returned to Peking; the imperial dogs came too, and remained exclusively imperial, at least until the Boxer rebellion of 1900. Even then, when the ladies of the foreign legations were unwillingly received by the Empress Tzŭ-hsi and asked to see her pekingese, she would say 'The naughty Boxers killed all my dogs', which was untrue: the butterfly lions were still cherished in the palaces.

The Empress had one especial pet which followed her wherever she went. Her lady-in-waiting of those last years, 'Princess' Der-ling, says, 'It has absolutely nothing to recommend it', but had to acknowledge it was next in importance to the Empress herself.

His name was Hai Lung, sea otter, because he so much resembled one of those animals. He was . . . dark brown, with long silky hair . . . small, bow-legged, snub-nosed, and had the biggest eyes of any dog I ever saw. He was probably the best pedigreed dog in the Middle Kingdom, and Her Majesty adored the little brute [it is evident that the Princess did not!] He had a special eunuch to wait on him and slept in a large basket, big enough for a baby, and the basket was up-holstered with bright red silk.

There have been doubts about Der-ling's position at the Imperial Court and it is probable she was not as close to the Empress as she claims; that Der-ling was the daughter of Lord Yü Keng, of the Manchu White Banner class and Minister to France from 1899–1902 seems borne out by her knowledge of Western life and even Sir Reginald Johnstone, tutor to the infant Emperor Pu-Yi, acknowledges that she acted as inter-preter for the Empress; there are, too, photographs of Der-ling, her mother and sister, walking with the Empress Tzŭ-hsi. Der-ling also could hardly have known, or even invented, the countless details of Court life shown in her books, *Two Years in the Forbidden City* and *Imperial Incense*, without being much in the palaces. Unfortunately she wrote in an over-romantic, often ungrammatical style and, probably, embroidered facts, but she excels in palace tittle-tattle and details which have fascination in their very triviality, and conjure up a vivid picture of the Empress. For instance, about the dog:

His harness was of red silk-covered leather, and under his neck were three bells, two small ones and one, the central one, somewhat larger. Every time the dog moved he made music of his own. On the back of his collar, just behind his ears, were two fluffy pompoms, one of red silk, the other of green. His leash was several feet in length, and was hung all along the length with tiny bells. One always knew when the dog-eunuch took his charge anywhere. When it trotted the bells could be heard for some distance.

The dog-eunuch prepared the animal's food – of

chopped liver mixed with rice and gravy – and took it
to Li Lien-ying, [the Chief Eunuch], who in turn took
it to Her Majesty for inspection. She was as careful of
the animal's food as of her own. If it did not suit, back
it went to the kitchen, with a scolding for the cook
. . . . If anything had ever happened to that dog it
would have upset the entire routine of the court!

Queen Victoria's love for her dogs was as deep, if not as
discriminating; as a girl, coming back from her coronation and
still cumbered by her robes, she had run upstairs to bath her
little spaniel Dash. She loved birds too: among the ornate dog
graves in Windsor Park, each with the dog's effigy cast in
bronze, is one grave so tiny it is easily missed. It is of Little
Bully, who for thirteen years was her favourite bullfinch.

This is an unexpected taste in an Englishwoman. The
Chinese had long had a predilection for caged singing birds –
elderly gentlemen, in particular, could be seen taking them for
evening walks, each on its stick or in its cage. The Empress
Tzŭ-hsi liked them free and had an uncanny power over them.
Katharine Carl, the artist, describes this power with something
like awe:

. . . On one of our promenades in the park I saw a
curious instance of her wonderful personal magnetism
and her power over animals. A bird had escaped from
its cage, and some eunuchs were making efforts to catch
it, when Her Majesty and suite came into that part of
the grounds. The eunuchs had found it impossible to
entice the bird back into its cage . . . the Empress
Dowager said, 'I will call it down'. I thought this was a
vain boast, and in my heart I pitied her. She was so
accustomed to have the whole world bow to her, she
fancied even a bird in the grounds would obey her man-

dates, and I watched to see how she would take her defeat. She had a long, wand-like stick, which had been cut from a sapling and freshly stripped of its bark . . . . She held the wand . . . aloft and made a low, bird-like sound with her lips, never taking her eyes off the bird. She had the most musical of voices, and its flute-like sound seemed like a magical magnet to the bird. He fluttered and began to descend from bough to bough until he lighted upon the crook of her wand, when she gently moved her other hand up nearer and nearer, until it finally rested on her finger . . . .

I saw another instance of her magnetic power, this time with a katydid [cricket]. One of the Princesses, seeing one on a bush, tried to catch it, but in vain. Her Majesty held out her hand toward the beautiful insect, made a peculiar sound like their own cry and advanced her outstretched finger until it rested upon it. She stroked it gently for a few moments, and then removed her fingers, and the katydid made no effort to fly until she put it down.

Princess Der-ling was more cynical than honest Miss Carl and recorded that the eunuchs had trained the birds to do this, but they could hardly have trained the katydid.

During the Manchu exile in Jehol the Emperor Hsien-fêng, partly from shame, partly from his own dissipations, had 'ascended the phoenix chariot and returned to the nine sources,' a description not suited to Prince Albert's death in December of 1861; both Queen Victoria and Tzŭ-hsi were widowed in the same year, a state that perfectly suited the Manchu but almost annihilated Queen Victoria.

The shadows had been darkening for her through the last two years with her mother's death, the worry over the behaviour of the Prince of Wales and, worst of all, Prince Albert's health and his failing response to the demands she so constantly made on him. These domestic troubles may explain her curious indifference to, even ignorance of, what was happening in Peking. 'This Chinese affair is vexatious', she had written but, to her, only vexatious – real tragedy was the sorrow at Windsor. What was thought a mere chill developed, with the already delicate Prince Consort into a 'putrid fever' – no one dared mention the word typhoid – and on Saturday, 14 December, he died in the Blue Room at the Castle.

The pitiful Chinese Emperor Hsien-fêng had not formally decreed who should succeed him and after his death there were violent wranglings and plots, but Tzŭ-hsi, though out of favour, had taken the precaution of spiriting away – it was said with the help of a favourite young eunuch – the most important of the Emperor's twenty-five seals, the Seal of Lawfully Transmitted Authority, by which she had the power to confirm her little son, Tsai-ch'un, as Emperor with herself and the Empress Niuhuru as Regents. Travelling in advance of the great funeral cortege they came back to Peking, though had it not been for the protection of the Manchu bannermen under Tzŭ-hsi's faithful cousin, Jung-lu, they would have been assassinated on the way. The new government was established, Tzŭ-hsi's chief opponents were given 'the silken cord' with which to hang themselves, so avoiding the disgrace of public execution.

The Little Emperor, to show that harmony had been restored, was given a new name, T'ung-chih – Return to Order.

Queen Victoria and the Empress Dowager, as Tzŭ-hsi was now known, were to rule as opposites, one in the far West, the other in the Far East, for more than forty years, Queen Victoria for a long while unwillingly, Tzŭ-hsi with relish.

All through those years, Queen Victoria seems to have remained almost in ignorance of her opposite Empress; perhaps her imagination, not at any time a vivid one, could not have stretched so far. We know that the Queen sent the Empress Tzŭ-hsi a musical box – from the time of the Jesuit clockmaker Ricci, the Chinese had been fascinated by Western mechanical tricks, just as the English had been fascinated by chinoiserie – but the Empress kept a photograph of the English Queen in her bedroom. 'I have heard much of Queen Victoria', she was to write. 'Still I don't think her life is half as interesting and eventful as mine . . .'.

She ruled though 'behind the yellow curtain', a veil in the Audience Halls that showed she presided only in the Emperor's name. T'ung-chih, it is true, came of age and ostensibly assumed the Dragon Throne; his mother, as ostensibly, retired, but, like his father the Emperor, T'ung-chih was so dissolute and weak that he was content to leave all political and government affairs in her hands. He died of smallpox at the age of nineteen, leaving no heir and, through the Empress Tzŭ-hsi's machinations, another baby emperor was chosen, Kuang-hsü, just three years old. Though he was her sister's son, the Empress adopted him as her own and so remained Regent.

> England is one of the great powers of the world, [she continued, writing of her opposite Queen] but this has not been brought about by Queen Victoria's absolute rule. She had the ablest of men of parliament back of her at all times . . . would sign the necessary documents and really had nothing to say about the policy of the country. Now look at me. I have 400,000,000 people dependent on my judgment . . . anything of an important nature I must decide myself.

Queen Victoria in middle age, painted by Lady Abercrombie

Entirely by herself. In 1881 her unobtrusive partner, the Empress Niuhuru, died. It is said that she had shown the Empress a document detrimental to her, Tzŭ-hsi, and then torn it up, but even to show it was enough; next day the Empress Tzŭ-hsi sent a present of milk cakes to her old friend. Niuhuru took a mouthful – it would have been a breach of etiquette to do anything else – but by the evening she was dead. There is no proof that this was Tzŭ-hsi's doing, any more than there is proof of innumerable tales of her ruthlessness and cruelty: for instance, that she ordered T'ung-chih's girl wife Alute to commit suicide after his death. We only know that Alute took an overdose of opium and died. For any true story there must be a hundred that are calumnies, but the Empress Tzŭ-hsi was certainly more than cruel to the second of her young emperors, Kuang-hsü; he had taken the throne in 1869, but she still kept the power to 'instruct' him, dismiss and appoint officials over his head and examine all state powers which in fact meant she had all authority.

In 1898, warned by the faithful Jung-lu, she discovered a plot to kill Jung-lu himself, then surround her palace and keep her prisoner while young Kuang-hsü assumed full power.

The Empress's army was strong and, by dawn on the appointed day, the Forbidden City was in her hands; Kuang-hsü was forced to abdicate and it was he who was imprisoned on an island of the Sea Palace. He was fetched back to escape with the Empress in the ignominious flight of the Boxer rebellion, and it was then that she gave her most terrible order of all; Kuang-hsü's favourite, the beautiful and spirited Pearl Concubine, pleaded with the Empress to remain with the Emperor and face the rabble; outraged, the Empress shouted to the eunuchs and the beautiful proud Pearl Concubine was thrown down a well to drown while the Emperor helplessly looked on.

The Empress Tzŭ-hsi had, of course, been brought up in a callous and fierce school; as a young Regent she had been forced to sign the death warrant for the same young eunuch who had stolen the late Emperor's Seal for her; not even she could save him. 'Have you ever been beaten?' she was to ask Princess Der-ling who, having been brought up in Europe, was not used to Chinese ways; but, as she grew older and more powerful, the Empress grew more irascible; everywhere she went, even to walk in her loved gardens, the dreaded bamboo canes, carried by two strong eunuchs went with her.

Queen Victoria had a hot temper too. 'It is my greatest burden', she had written as a girl and, 'There is often an irritability in me that makes me say cross and odious things', but it seems that the nearest she approached to violence was when she threw a cup of tea in Prince Albert's face, spoiling his cravat – and Albert took pride in his clothes. 'Victoria is too hasty and passionate for me to be able to speak of my difficulties', he wrote to Stockmar, his wise old confidant.

Tzŭ-hsi painted by the American artist Katharine Carl

'She will not hear me out but flies into rages . . .'

In the end Albert won, but the Empress Tzŭ-hsi had no husband to curb her in any way. 'A combination of Catherine [the Great of Russia] and Semiramis,' Lord Salisbury was to call her which was near truth, yet she and the staid Queen Victoria were counterparts, not only in position, but in person; both were diminutive, Tzŭ-hsi just five feet tall, though in her Manchu shoes she stood six inches taller. Queen Victoria, to her grief, was under five feet. 'Everybody grows but me', she had lamented as a girl, but both quickly developed that magnetic power of authority that could quell with a look.

They kept that power, though as they grew older both grew plump and plain. Even face powder was outré in Victorian court circles and in China, as in India, widows were forbidden to make up – but in this the Empress Tzŭ-hsi was defiant, saying she was following the Confucian maxim 'Cultivate your person'. She dyed her hair which was dressed every morning in the elaborate Manchu way, a nerve-racking ordeal for the eunuch in charge; not a hair must be pulled out or tweaked. Her rouge was made of pure rose petals, her lotions distilled from honeysuckle, but her cleansing cream was not as romantic – it was pure mutton fat.

One thing, though, remained beautiful all their lives; both had musical voices, Queen Victoria's exceptionally sweet and low, and both had 'carriage', dignity in the way they moved.

After Prince Albert died Queen Victoria spent little on clothes but as a girl she had loved them. Her Aunt Louise, Queen of the Belgians, who had not much opinion of the Duchess of Kent's taste, had sent dresses and bonnets from Paris, but it was Mrs Louis, 'Old Louie', once dresser to her ill-fated cousin, Princess Charlotte, who really taught young Victoria the astounding effects that could be made by dignity and grace even when beauty was absent.

The Empress Tzŭ-hsi's clothes, being loose oriental robes, never went out of fashion or ceased to fit her, yet new ones were made, if not every week, every month of each year. As she moved from palace to palace her wardrobe was carried in wicker trays, padded with imperial yellow, each dress a poem: there was the 'dress of a thousand butterflies': another with phoenixes embroidered with pearls: a 'simple' dress was woven of grey and pink raw silk which gave it a changeable light as she moved. When Princess Der-ling travelled with the Empress to Manchuria only garments suitable for spring and summer were taken – two thousand dresses.

The Chinese court had its own silk weavers, indeed its own silkworms; there were embroiderers, tailors, craftsmen of every kind. Ten women made the Empress's shoes in myriad designs from plum blossom to phoenixes and dragons, some with as many as five hundred seed pearls, some using only twenty, but all different. By contrast Queen Victoria's hand-made black shoes were plain – the famous firm of Joseph Lobb still has her 'lasts', surprisingly small, as were her dresses – one, in the black bombazine she wore most, with fine white edging at the sleeves and neck can be seen in the London Museum. 'My dress is always the same', she wrote to Dearest Child, 'as it is the dress I have adopted for ever as mine'. In other words, a widow's, though they could hardly have been called weeds. 'I had a long veil to my cap which was trimmed with large diamonds . . . and the last time with large pearls.'

Queen Victoria loved jewellery and was given superb pieces, particularly by the Indian Maharajahs when she became their Empress, and also had handsome presents from the Kimberley mines. Sir Ponsonby Fane, as Lord Chamberlain, wrote to their directors in 1891,

The first-rank concubine's winter crown and elaborately jewelled nail protectors

The Queen has selected two stones to keep as specimens of your mine at Kimberley and Her Majesty desires
me to thank you very sincerely for this valuable present
. . . and appreciates the loyal feeling that prompted you
to offer them.

Anyone who visits the Tower of London can see the splendour
of the Crown Jewels, though these, of course were not her own.

The Empress Tzŭ-hsi had few valuable stones, diamonds
emeralds or sapphires; nor did she wear rubies though these
must have been found in China as a ruby button was granted to
ornament the hat of mandarins and officials of the highest rank.

The Chinese imperial jewel was the pearl; no one but the
Emperor was allowed to wear the symbol of the Flaming
Pearl but, on official occasions, the Empress wore the renowned pearl cape 'made of more than three thousand pearls,
the size of a canary bird's egg, all exactly alike in colour and
perfectly round: it was made in a fish-net pattern, had a fringe
of jade pendants and was fastened with two jade clasps.'
Strings of pearls always hung from her headdress.

How elaborate the beautiful lady's coiffure!
What lovely pearls and emerald jades on her head!
Does she realise that the two specks of cloud she wears
Wear out the taxes of several villages?

Jade was the most precious of the semi-precious stones for
which China was famous, far more prized than her coral, tour-
maline, crystal, turquoise or amethyst; its great attraction was
not only its beauty but its 'virtue'.

'Why is jade so valuable, Master?' one of his disciples asked Confucius, to which the Master replied: 'From time immemorial, men have found in jade all the virtues. For is it not soft, smooth and shining like benevolence? Moreover, it is beautiful, robust and compact, like intelligence; it has sharp, but not cutting, edges, like justice, and when it is struck, it emits a long, clear note. It does not try to hide its defects, which do but enhance its beauty, like sincerity. And its substance, found in the mountains and the torrents, shines like the heavens. It is therefore right that all should love it, as all should love duty and truth'.

The Empress Tzŭ-hsi knew her Confucius, from those early years of waiting when, a humble concubine, she had studied the classics; she wrote her own poems – not for her the diaries and 'leaves' from domestic happenings written by the English Queen. She would have despised the simple straight-forward way in which Queen Victoria described Scotland and particularly Balmoral, her Scottish retreat.

The sun cast a glorious light and the surrounding hills which were quite pink gave a crimson hue to the heather on the moor below. The sky was pink and lilac and pale green and became richer and richer while the hills in the other direction were of deep blue. It was wonder-fully beautiful . . . .

It was not only the beauty, it was the peace the Queen loved. 'No crowd, no trouble or annoyance . . . this solitude, the romance and wild loveliness . . . the absence of hotels and beggars . . .' She loved the pure air and quiet, 'the simple mountaineers', from whom she learned many a lesson of resig-nation and faith.

Queen Victoria had discovered and fallen in love with the Highlands in 1842 when, on her first visit to Scotland with Prince Albert, they had stayed at Tayworth Castle. In 1852, with an unexpected fortune left her by an eccentric old miser, she was able to buy and largely rebuild the castle of Balmoral, 'in Scottish baronial style with turrets and pepper-pots'.

Balmoral Castle

In spite of its beautiful surroundings, Balmoral could hardly have been more hideous in its heavy ornateness, its tartan wallpapers and carpets – 'the thistles were worse than the plaids', as Lord Clarendon said. It was also a bitterly cold house; fires were few and far between – the Queen hated warm rooms: 'I always feel so brisk in cold weather', which is more than her shivering ladies did. Balmoral to her was heaven. 'Every year', she wrote, 'my heart becomes more fixed in this paradise', but, after each 'deliverance', she had to go back to what she called 'that dungeon Windsor'.

The Empress Tzŭ-hsi too hated her Peking palace in the Forbidden City. 'There is nothing in it but vast buildings, empty save for echoes. Except for the Imperial Gardens there are no flowers', and one suspects these gardens were formal, 'no fresh breezes. The place is so cold. It has no heart'.

It would seem that every Chinese Dynasty ended in ruin because of its rulers' passion for making extravagant gardens: the Empress Tzŭ-hsi and the Ch'ing Dynasty followed the pattern. When the second of her Emperor charges, Kuang-hsü, reached his majority she had issued a seemingly innocent decree. It read: 'In the neighbourhood [of Peking] there was a palace' – she had long since seen to it that she had been given the site. 'Many of the buildings . . . only require some reconstruction to make it a place of solace and delight'. This was, she added pathetically, for her retirement, which she never made. It was the old Summer Palace and it was true that a few of the buildings had escaped the barbarian burnings; the Bronze Temple still stood as did the Jade Girdle Bridge which, with its reflection in the water, made a perfect circle.

'The costs of reconstruction have all been provided for', said the decree. 'Out of surplus funds accumulated as a result of rigid economy. No harm will be done to the national finances' – only seventy million taels from the Admiralty which had been set aside for the modernising of the fleet. The only boat built with the money was the marble picnic boat that floated on the Summer Palace lake and, from the navy's weakness, China lost the war with Japan and the Ch'ing Dynasty was overthrown.

The Empress though had no regrets. 'Here is loveliness', she said. 'There is room to walk, to look. This is our home'.

Even with that amount of money she could not rebuild the whole – only use the site, a little removed from the ruins, of what used to be the Garden of Clear Rippling Waters, with its Hill of Tranquil Longevity or Ten Thousand Years Hill, and lake, bridges, pavilions and pagodas.

The only flowers Queen Victoria seems to have liked were snowdrops, primroses and heather. The Chinese did not encourage wild flowers and in cultivating them went to extremes. 'An official might summon his friends to admire a mauve chrysanthemum, its petals meticulously curled each morning with chopsticks. All the lesser buds would have been stripped off so that the vital force was concentrated on this single flower, and in the corner of the garden there would be a shrine dedicated to the buds which had been sacrificed'. For these flower gatherings the etiquette was rigid, even the dress pre-

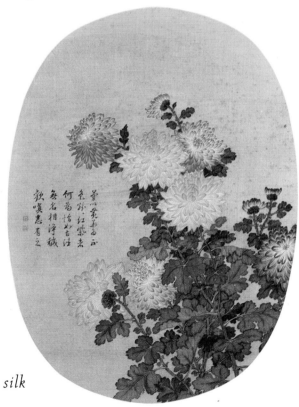

Chrysanthemum scroll in silk

scribed; the silks were to be sufficiently rich to honour the flowers, yet not so gay as to eclipse them.

In the Empress Tzŭ-hsi's Summer Palace, like Ch'ien-lung's far larger one, the peony terraces were most beautiful of all; the deeper coloured flowers were planted near the Lake shore and were shaded up the hill to those of the lightest shades so that 'they gave the illusion of a landscape fading into the distance'. They were all tree paeonies – the Chinese would have despised our bunched garden kinds – and it was so important they should bloom for the Empress's birthday that the gardeners would light small fires along the terraces and sit up all night to keep them burning and bring on the buds.

Queen Victoria, one suspects, would have dismissed such ideas as extravagant and fanciful – but perhaps it was the lack of 'fancies', of delight in life, that made the days at Balmoral so dull, even for her. Loud talk and laughter were forbidden, no one was allowed to go out of doors until the Queen went; etiquette was strictly observed. 'Putting grumbling aside, the life here is utterly boring', wrote Marie Mallet, a favourite maid-of-honour. 'The weather is horribly cold and wet . . . we just exist from meal to meal and do our best to kill time. We had a ladies' dinner last night. The Queen wore jet and hardly uttered.'

The meals seemed to have been endless. The Queen breakfasted in her room with one of the Princesses. Luncheon was at two, tea at five-thirty, then came dressing for dinner, which was at nine, if with the Queen, at a quarter-to if with the Household. All of them were hearty meals but Queen Victoria gobbled, so that as soon as she had finished everyone's plates were whisked away.

No one ate with the Empress Tzŭ-hsi; in fact, her ladies had to stand while she was at table. For breakfast she had lotus-root porridge and milk — Princess Der-ling insists that it was human milk from the wives of Manchu soldiers, kept in the palaces for this purpose. There were always at least a hundred dishes at luncheon and dinner, and each meal began with sweets, seeds, nuts and fruit of which the Empress ate an enormous quantity. Beef was taboo but all sorts of game appeared and that speciality, pork, which she loved. Then there was stuffed melon, crystallized bamboo shoots and ginger, bread in fancy shapes, pickles, sugar-cane syrup . . . more sweet porridge. It was no wonder that after luncheon the Empress sank into somnolence until five o'clock. It is said that her pekingese, which were released into the marble courtyards to play at this time, were bred with feathered feet, which they still have, so that they did not disturb the silence of her siesta.

In the Summer Palace, as she wandered about the grounds or picnicked in the marble boat on the lake, a travelling kitchen went with her, as did musicians. The Chief Eunuch, Li Lien-ying, was at her right side whether she walked or rode in her chair; four eunuchs of the fifth rank went before, twelve of the sixth rank behind and each carried something; shoes, handkerchiefs; combs and brushes; powder boxes; looking glasses; pins; pen, ink and paper in case she might wish to write a poem; one eunuch had her yellow satin stool. Besides these there were two amahs and four lesser servant girls again each carrying something. It made Princess Der-ling think 'of a lady's dressing-table on legs'. Every day this procession, with the uniforms of the eunuchs, the delicate colours and gorgeous silks of the ladies, the embroideries and coloured lacquers, the swaying tasselled umbrellas, wound its brilliant way through the beauties of the gardens.

All festivals were kept, lending interest and harmless enjoyment to the whole year; the Feast of Lanterns: the Autumn

Festival: the New Year when hangings and scrolls were changed throughout the palaces and there were carnivals and firework displays.

It is sad to think how much, as a young girl, Queen Victoria had loved gaiety, colour and dancing. In those days she had had a zest for pleasure that, though she would have been shocked to know it, was a legacy from her disgraceful royal uncles, especially Prinny, but Albert seems to have taken that zest away – and the laughter; Coburgs did not smile! And her natural warm-heartedness was buried under the royal dignity and etiquette he had instilled; even at Balmoral it was rigidly observed; 'Old gentlemen with gout were kept standing for hours after dinner . . .' The only diversions seem to have been occasional concerts and ghillies' balls – in all weathers – the Queen went out in all weathers too.

That both Empresses did their duty is unassailable; Queen Victoria's 'boxes', those despatches and letters, were present no matter where she went, even on holiday, even on the honeymoon for which Prince Albert had hoped. 'You forget, my dearest love, I am the Sovereign, and that business can stop and wait for nothing.' She felt the cruel edge of this in her widowhood. For the Empress Tzŭ-hsi there were the long daily audiences which began soon after dawn – it was the unpleasant duty of one of the court ladies to wake her – and risk her temper.

And both Empresses had their dogs. Queen Victoria seems to have chosen hers at random with no regard for a particular breed or looks; there was Dash, the little spaniel of her teens and, just before she married, she wrote to Albert saying she had been given a Scottish terrier called Laddie. 'You will be smothered in dogs', she had warned the Prince. On that two-day honeymoon they were accompanied by a greyhound, Eos:

'he was black with a silver streak and his name meant Dawn'. That was the nearest she came to a poetical name: the rest were Spot, Laddie, Sharp, Noble, names as basically simple and undiscriminating as herself; she seems to have felt no shame at Lootie's incriminating name, and what would she have said to the Chinese Cha hua – Tea Blossom; Hing-chen – Star Dust; Hun-heng – Pugnacious; Lo-tse – Bit of Joy. Pekingese lend themselves to poetry but sometimes, in their search for differences, the breeders go too far. The kennel name of one of mine is Radiant Light of Alderbourne, and when he first came, 'I'm not going to call "Radiant! Radiant" up the street', said my husband.

Every sort of dog seems to have made its way to Windsor and often many years in advance of its appearance elsewhere in the West: there were Saint Bernards, Pyrenean sheepdogs, Italian mountain sheepdogs, Pomeranian, Russian, German and Italian greyhounds, Maltese – far too many to keep as palace pets; the royal kennels were necessary. Some of the dogs came from a British victory overseas, as Lootie did; there was Cashmere, a Tibetan mastiff, the white fluffy Chico and Goliath from the Cuban insurrection. Many of these were painted by Landseer and Charles Burton Barber. The Queen used to drive down to the kennels in her pony carriage to the Queen's Cottage that still stands in the park, though the kennels are gone. The cottage had prim little flowerbeds and windows overgrown with honeysuckle. One was known as the Queen's window as she used to sit there and watch the dogs brought out to romp and play in view of the sitting room which she had made her own. Though they were not household pets she knew them all – this was long after the days of Lootie. With her dogs the Queen could be as warm hearted as she felt and one guesses she could have loved even a mongrel.

Not so the Empress Tzŭ-hsi; all her life she kept to her
chosen breed and of that only the peers. 'Her Majesty seldom
walked around Ten Thousand Years Hill', the Princess wrote,
without visiting the kennels which, at the Summer Palace, were
bamboo cages in a separate courtyard.

When we were almost at the kennels the eunuch in
charge called out 'Lao Fo Yea li la!' meaning, 'Old
Buddha arrives!' . . . and such a commotion as that
caused! The dogs all began to run swiftly about their
cages, barking loudly, plainly very happy to see Her
Majesty. Old Buddha was pleased with them . . . . When
we stood before the kennels the eunuchs loosed the dogs
from their cages and called out: 'Ta guerh!' and every
dog in the kennels that was big enough began to turn
somersaults in the courtyard, barking and lolling out
his tongue. Then the eunuch spoke again. 'Tzan tzu!'
which is equivalent to the military term 'Fall in'. All
the dogs lined up before the court retinue, their bulging
eyes, full of intelligence, peering out at Her Majesty
. . . . When all the dogs were lined up, and perfectly
still – they would bark or remain silent at command –
the eunuch called out again:
   'Chi li!' which means 'stand up'. Then all the dogs
sat on their haunches and waited, still with red
tongues lolling. Of course some of them were awkward
and had to keep trying, and the eunuch waited until
all were erect, when he spoke sharply, again:
   'Ga Lao Fo Yea, bai bai!' which meant something
like 'give greetings to Her Majesty, the Old Buddha'.
The dogs barked and waved their front feet as though
waving them at Her Majesty.

. . . If Her Majesty wished to examine one of the dogs closer she would indicate which one and the eunuch would hold the animal up for her inspection. Then she would say, 'Its eyes are dirty; you must take better care of it', or, 'Its hind legs are not of the right length', or, 'Its body is too long'. Whenever she commented thus on any dog, especially the puppies, it was a decree of exile – for it meant the dog had to be taken away.

Miss Carl has described them playing in the courtyards: 'When the Court was taking its siesta, I used to go out to where the dogs were basking in the sun in their own court' – a marble pavilion near the Empress's own – 'and look at and play with these interesting little animals'.

Pekingese playing on a lawn, as they did at Lord John Hay's Fulmer Place, give a quality to the garden as do peacocks and swans. For a while in India I lived on a teagarden where the terraces fell one below the other from the bungalow to the river. I had nine pekingese then and every afternoon they would run down to the river, tails waving, ear-feathers flying among the bushes of tea.

The West has given one thing to these little dogs which they had not had in China, at any rate since the sixth century, and that is sport. Shampoo, a pekingese bitch who lives in Scotland, retrieves trout for her owner; though small, she will get a six-pound trout and once, when a little one was flung on the bank, she carried it after her mistress, jumping the heather and holding the trout, head in, tail forward, the only way her flat-shaped mouth could carry a limp long thing. She does every-thing her companion, a labrador, does and, in a fast-running river, holds on to the labrador's tail to prevent herself being washed down. 'Pekingese are so sensible', their proud owners say. Shampoo certainly is, but bravado can oust sense. That first one of mine, Piers, loved sailing, but my father did not like having him on board as he was often seasick and, while we were on holiday in Wales, I had strict orders to shut him up when we went sailing on the Milford Haven. Piers though had a genius for escaping and often I would look back and see a small black head following us straight out to the Atlantic.

They have extraordinary powers of endurance. My sister, who had also succumbed to the lure of pekingese, had, in India, a golden pekingese called Leo. True he was large but even so . . . . She went up to the foothills to stay in a remote bungalow with a forest officer and his wife, owners of a bull-terrier and a hefty springer spaniel. One evening they were walking on the edge of deep jungle when a troop of monkeys was startled out of the trees, fleeing into the jungle. The dogs, including Leo, went after them, and, in spite of commands, shouts, cries, vanished. It was just upon dusk. Apart from any-thing else, monkeys, in numbers, are mischievous with dogs, more than mischievous, malicious and tormenting; the Indian jungle is thick, heavy with creepers, underbush, thorns, and Leo had a long thick coat. 'The others might get through but a pekingese – in any case he could not keep up . . .' The forest officer and his wife gently took my sister away to the bungalow. 'Besides, there are lynx, wild dog, worst of all, leopard. I don't think you will see Leo again'.

Hours after, about ten o'clock, there was a scratching at the forest bungalow door; there was the bull terrier, battered, with a bloody eye; the springer, his coat entangled with leaves, grass, thorns and, between them, exhausted but intrepid, Leo.

Of course not all pekingese are sporting – any more than humans; bitches, especially, can be most sybaritic. Such a one was Silk, well-named; she was silken, honey-coloured with

white and sepia touches and great eyes that she would blink
eloquently when she wanted anything – which she usually did.
Never was there a prettier coquette. She had a passion for men
which was usually returned; my husband was besotted about
her – I think he only married me to become the owner of
Silk – I was merely the handmaid who waited on her, groomed
and fed her and was useful in illness or stress.

She always had her own way; if she wished to go no further
on a walk she would sit down and, even if we went on for a
mile, would not move – she knew eventually we should be
compelled to come back and fetch her. Food not to her taste
she would not touch; in fact would rather starve than eat what
she did not like; we once tried for ten days – I wish Sir
Charles Phipps could have met Silk. When she had puppies,
the only time – 'Never again', I said – she screamed like a
prima donna. Pekingese are usually devoted mothers: a little
bitch I know had her litter in a converted chicken-house that
caught fire; one by one she brought her puppies out, and had
to be prevented from going back for the last when the whole
house was in flames. Silk deserted her puppies on the third day.

Yet she gave my husband at least twelve years of delight and
amusement; in the early morning, after I had got up and let
her out, she would jump on his bed, steal up, sit on his chest
and gently touch his eyelids with her paw until he opened
them. In the evening she would hear the car long before I
could and would wait and whine at the front door.

On Dash's grave Queen Victoria had ordered to be in-
scribed three lines which perhaps tell more than she realised:

His attachment was without selfishness
His playfulness without malice
His fidelity without deceit

Court life, in any country, is seldom free of intrigue or, at the least, self-interest; of jockeying for position, for profit in some form or another; the two Queens must often have felt a weariness of people, and the innocent love of their dogs must have been a true relief.

Queen Victoria did inspire true love and loyalty, especially in her later years, as Marie Mallet describes:

> The darling Queen . . . . I have been with the Queen twice today and she was more angelic than ever. I think I am a little bit of use and comfort to her and that rejoices me more than anything. When she breaks down she draws me close to her and lets me stroke her dear hands.

The Empress Tzŭ-hsi was too alarming for that. Her eunuchs cheated her in ways that were shaming; of the necessary hundred dishes served for luncheon or dinner, those that she did not favour, and the cooks were sure she would not eat, were served up again and again until they were full of weevils; now and again she was moved to give, with her chop-sticks, a tidbit to a favourite lady or maid which the shrinking victim had to take and eat. Every year on her birthday she released a thousand of the caged birds the Chinese were so fond of keeping. She believed she had set them free but, out of her sight, the eunuchs, scrambling up the trees with nets and sticks, caught them again and sold them in the markets. Even Princess Der-ling, for all her protestations, has passages in her books about the Empress that are, if not spiteful, cynical. The only person the Old Buddha could trust absolutely was her Chief Eunuch, Li Lien-ying, because his interests were bound up with her own.

He shared her love of pekingese and was one of the few commoners allowed to own them, but when his house was burned down he lost his three special favourites in the fire. Li Lien-ying was enormously rich and, in memory of them, he had three snuff bottles made of finest porcelain: priceless in their beauty, each was painted with one of the dogs and the symbol of its name: Sung To – Pine Cone; Chu Yeh – Bamboo Leaf; Mei Ha – Plum Flower. The plum tree flowers in winter while the bamboo and pine are evergreen so that all three are symbols of fidelity. Li Lien-ying never forgot his little dogs.

To be set on any pinnacle is lonely; that of those two Empresses was so high they had no equal, except one another, and they were strangers on opposite sides of the world. Loneliness brings a sore heart and, if one's heart is sore, it is marvellous how much balm a dog's love can bring.

Agate snuff bottle with amber pekingese

CHAPTER FIVE

Points and Pearls

LET THE LION DOG BE SMALL;
Let it wear the swelling cape of dignity around its neck;
Let it bear the billowing standard of pomp above its back.

Let its face be black;
Let its forefront be shaggy;
Let its forehead be straight and low,
Like unto the brow of an Imperial harmony boxer.

Let its eyes be large and luminous;
Let its ears be set like the sails of a war junk;
Let its nose be like that of the Monkey God of the Hindus.

Let its forelegs be bent
So that it shall not desire to wander far,
Or leave the Imperial Precincts.

Let its body be shaped
Like that of the hunting lion spying for its prey;

Let its feet be tufted
With plentiful hair that its footfall may be soundless;
And for its standard of pomp,
Let it rival the whisk of the Tibetan yak,
Which is flourished to protect the Imperial litter
From the attacks of flying insects.

Let it be lively,
That it may afford entertainment by its gambols;
Let it be discreet
That it may not involve itself in danger;
Let it be friendly in its habits,
That it may live in amity with the other beasts,
Fishes, or birds that find protection in the Imperial Palace.

And for its colour
Let it be that of a lion – a golden sable,

To be carried in the sleeve of a yellow robe,
Or the colour of a red bear
Or of a black bear, or a white bear, or striped like a dragon
So that there may be dogs appropriate to each of the Imperial
   robes.

Let it venerate its ancestors
And deposit offerings in the dog cemetery
Of the Forbidden City on each New Moon,
Let it comport itself with dignity,
Let it learn to bite the foreign devils instantly.

Let it be dainty in its food
That it shall be known as an Imperial dog
By its fastidiousness.

Sharks' fins
And curlews' livers
And the breasts of quails, on these it may be fed.

And for drink
Give it tea that is brewed from the spring buds
Of the shrub that grows in the province of Hankow,
Or the milk of the antelopes
That pasture in the Imperial Parks.

Thus shall it preserve its integrity and self-respect;
And for the day of sickness let it be anointed
With the clarified fat of the leg of a sacred leopard,
And give it to drink a throstle's eggshell full of the juice
Of a custard apple in which has been dissolved three pinches
Of shredded rhinoceros horn, and apply to it piebald leeches.

So shall it remain – but if it die,
Remember, that thou too art mortal!

These are the Pearls Dropped from the Lips Of Her Imperial Majesty Tzŭ-Hsi Dowager Empress of the Flowery Land of Confucius.

She ruled now without the yellow curtain. After the Boxer rebellion the second young Emperor, Kuang-hsü, ill and lonely, no longer seemed to care either for himself or his country and the Empress Tzŭ-hsi's rule was absolute.

Even as children both the unfortunate little boys, Kuang-hsü and, before him, T'ung-chih had been forced to sit quietly in all their panoply through the long hours of the morning Audiences. Had the Empress ever been fond of them? Perhaps of her real son? Princess Der-ling tells of a ritual visit to the 'relics of the Eight Emperors', among them the Empress's husband, Hsien-fêng and that son, T'ung-chih.

Queen Victoria had kept Prince Albert's room, the Blue Room at Windsor, exactly as it was, except for a bust between the beds, wreaths and palm branches on them. Bishop Davidson was distressed to find that when some thirty years later, she received him in Prince Albert's dressing-room at Balmoral before dinner, a footman brought in hot water and a clean towel 'for the ghost of the dear departed'. Victorians were sentimental over deathbeds but this was excessive morbidity; the Chinese ancestor worship seemed better to fit the dead into their place, revered, honoured, but gone; Princess Der-ling tells how, the Empress paused to look at T'ung-chih's gold bowl, his coronation robe embroidered with dragons.

That tiny robe of imperial yellow and the little blue satin collar studded with pearls; the two cases filled with his toys, bows and arrows . . . his diabolo, his bronze drum, silent now and, most touching of all, a white plaster rabbit which had a string in its back; when it was pulled, the rabbit's eyes moved and it shot forth a little red tongue. The Empress ordered it to be lifted from its case and kept it a long time in her hands.

She, too, must have longed to escape to her toys – to her flowers and birds and dogs. 'Black Jade has had four puppies', an eunuch announced before an important Audience and the Princess tells how the Empress's eyes brightened and how, though the audience was conducted with scrupulous observance, 'Her Majesty's mind ran more to dogs than matters of state'.

The Pearls, like the story of the shuttered pavilion and dead court lady, appear in every book (except Collier) about pekingese, but it is doubtful that the Empress really wrote them or, if indeed they dropped from her lips, they must have been embroidered into chinoiserie. Though the Chinese have a gift for inventing fanciful names and phrases for happenings, their writing in poems and documents is direct and spare, while the Pearls are wordy as well as ornate and flowery and there are extravagances that someone as sensible as the Empress over animals would surely not have countenanced; for instance, we know from Chinese history that the royal dogs, even the absurd Ling-ti's pet that wore the hat, were fed only on choice meat and rice; curlews abound in China along the shores of the Gulf of Pechale and there are plenty of quails, but a diet of them would have been far too rich for pekingese who are inclined to be livery dogs; leopards were not sacred in China nor leeches piebald – though there is such a creature as a white patched snail.

A pekingese, painted by Tsugouhara Foujita

No one knows where the Pearls really came from; it is told that, in fact, they were brought to England at the beginning of this century by a woman who had been in China for many years and written several books set there. This might have been Mrs Archibald Little who lived many years in China and wrote several books including *Intimate China* and *Round About My Peking Garden*. She may even have written the Pearls herself. Ellic Howe, of *The Pekingese Scrapbook*, advertised in *The Sunday*

Times for enlightenment about the Pearls with no result though he had one Chinese – modern – answer:

> Not only is the book [sic] ideologically banned as a relic of parasitic luxury in the People's Republic; not only will any copies in Japan be mysteriously unavailable on acknowledged grounds of sacrilege in the phrasing of the title [Why sacrilege, one wonders?] but the most optimistic mandarin in Formosa will feel the time involved in getting the book to London better occupied in annotating his copies of . . .

The last word was illegible but Ellic Howe was put firmly in his place; yet, authentic or not, the Pearls were taken up enthusiastically by some of the breeders and have given amusement to hundreds of people – as they do to me.

Of 'dogs in colours appropriate to the Imperial robes', the books also say that the Empress had dogs bred to match not only her robes but the flowers in her gardens – especially paeonies. If they had said 'chrysanthemums', with their bronze and yellow and cream, perhaps – but paeonies are purple, crimson, pink, and how could this have been done? The rare parti-colour of the lemon and white dogs are the nearest one can think of, but the Chinese did not like white – it is their colour of mourning.

Fortunately we know from V.W.F. Collier and his Chinese sources what were the real points of the original pekingese.

There were, in fact, three categories of dog in old China; those treasured 'under the table' dogs, hunting dogs similar to greyhounds or Tibetan mastiffs and the poor edible dogs, very like a chow. 'We saw pennes full of little dogs to sell', wrote

A very finely carved Japanese ivory model of a pekingese with a butterfly on its tail

one earlier traveller and, '. . . infinite number of Dogs are eaten in China', said another;

> they count their flesh delicate and nourishing, and have Butchers and Shambles where it is sold; . . . it is comical to see what a multitude of dogs pursue these butchers as they go along the Streets; I suppose the smell of the Dogs' flesh they carry about them provoke the other dogs. When they go loaded with half a dozen or more Dogs to the Shambles, the sport is still better; for the noise those so carry'd make, brings out all the Dogs in the Town to take their parts, and attack their mortal enemies.
>
> Black dogs are considered to be the most nutritious. 'Flowery dogs' – those of mixed colours – are reputed to be the most palatable, those of yellow and white colour following them in culinary value. The puppies are fattened on rice, and killed at an age of about nine months. After removing the hair by scalding, the body is cut into six or eight pieces and boiled for about an hour. It is then fried in oil. The meat is cut into small pieces and cooked with dry mushrooms, preserved bean-

cake, native onion, a little ginger, and water-chestnuts. The dish resulting is said to be exceedingly palatable, and to have the property of reducing fatigue due to sleepless-ness. For this reason the dish was very popular with students in the provincial and national examinations of the Manchu regime, which were carried on con-tinuously for several days.

Small dogs were also used in medicine and magic, curing not only youths of love-sickness but also of acne; 'the bodies of dead dogs were hung up in the shops with cats, mice, lizards and living birds with their eyes sewn up' — there is no doubt that the Chinese were cruel. The palace dogs may have heard the howling and barking as the butchers and sorcerers carried unlucky lesser dogs to the slaughter houses, but they had nothing to fear. They were far too precious.

It seems the favourite colours for them in China, besides the 'flowered' or parti-coloured pekingese in which the two colours had to be evenly distributed, were apricot-gold varying to a rich orange-red, the liver and the black. (It is ironic that the Pekin Palace Dog Association, when it split from the Pekingese Club, did not recognise 'liver-coloured pekingese', nor does the present-day British Kennel Club. It is not banned in America.) Best of all were any that had the markings of the Buddha. Among the marks were 'the tongue large and long,' but this led to some breeders trying to stretch a puppy's tongue which only resulted in its hanging from the middle of the mouth — a bad point as a good pekingese carries its tongue 'a little to the left or right'; a tongue too long was called by the Chinese 'a strangled ghost'.

Buddha also had, to distinguish him from other humans, the jaws of a lion, the upper part of the body also of a lion, a skin having a tinge of golden colour and, between the eye-brows, 'a little ball shining like snow,' forerunner perhaps of the mark of rank among officials – that button worn in front of the hat; in dogs it was often accompanied by a 'feather' or a blaze. As we have seen, Lootie had this, as has my own miniature Jade Button.

The tortoiseshell face was liked because it simulated laughter, also the 'three-flower face' which is a black 'mask' with a golden forehead and white round the mouth – most Alderbourne pekingese have a white mark under the chin; a black mask was prized if it went with another coloured, or mixed colour body, and some of the shaded colours, the sables and brindles, are beautiful. When Doctor Vlasto, the pekingese expert of the twenties, first saw a 'chun' or dark red pekingese – the famous Goodwood Chun, he wrote:

In those days I didn't know a pekingese from a sewing machine and it was the colour that caught my eye. Any ordinary dark red or mahogany dog is called a 'chun red' today but . . . as I recollect . . . he was like the best bits of colour on a ripe horse-chestnut with a coppery metallic sheen . . . which had a magnificent effect in sunlight.

The Alderbourne Kennel once bred a blue pekingese; news-papers everywhere reported it saying, 'If it does not change from blue it is likely to be priceless. Experts believe it will stay blue for it has a blue nose which is usually a reliable indication. It also has dark blue eyes and is pale fawn on chest and paws'. It was called Rhapsody in Blue. Miss Ashton Cross had a letter simply addressed, 'To the owner of the Blue Pekingese, England'. Blue Rhapsody was eventually sold to Prince Aly

Khan for the record price for a three-months-old puppy of a thousand pounds.

The Chinese distinguished between two distinct types of head – the apple ('p'ing kuo') or dome-shaped, and the abacus-shaped ('suan p'an tze-erh'). First-rate specimens of either type were held in equal estimation. The abacus is the Chinese counting-board, a frame strung with sliding beads, and the shape of the abacus ball may be reproduced by cutting off about one-fourth of its width from opposite sides of a wooden sphere, giving a flat top; this gave rise to the western insistence on a flat head for pekingese.

The ideal was to have 'the eyes so far apart and the tip of nose and forehead so much in the same plane that a silver dollar [about the size of our old half-crown] will, if lying flat on the plane of the dog's nostrils, touch the forehead, and at the same time lie at its broadest between, and not covering, any part of the eyes'. The Chinese description of this type of face was 'knife-cut mouth' . . . The best shape for the tip of the nose was that of the 'Ru-yi', a Buddhist emblem in the nature of a sceptre. The name refers to the boss at the end of the 'Ru-yi', which is very similar to another and rather more fixed standard of shape, that of the Chinese conventional cloud. This latter is the nose outline found in most of the bronze Chinese lion dogs.

To achieve this, horrific things are said to have been done; ignorant breeders, for instance, broke the cartilage of the nose with a chop-stick when the puppy was three weeks old, but a Dr J. E. Gray, writing in 1867, reported these were only tales, this from his findings on the typical skull that is in the British Museum; 'for the bones of the upper jaw and the nose are quite regular and similar on both sides, showing no forced distortion of any kind, such as is to be observed in the skulls of some Bull-dogs'. All the same, there was distortion; some of the breeders fed their puppies from a flat plate or taught them to bite pigskin stretched on a board, and puppies' noses were massaged every day to keep them flat.

The Chinese believed that a pekingese's ears should be placed well behind the middle axis of the forehead, not too high on the skull, and should be well feathered (not turned outwards in front) or projecting at the side. Other bad points occasionally found in China were sesame-seed, or prick, ears.

The mouth and cheeks might be round 'like dumplings', and never undershot – 'earth covers the heaven'. What would those breeders have said to my Piers?

They likened the eyes of their best specimens to the 'dragon-eye fish' or goldfish. Eyes they said should be large, lustrous and prominent, with the iris broad and of old-gold colour – water chestnut eyes. If showing rather more white they were called 'leopard-eyes', and often meant bad temper.

Ideal body development – next in importance to that of the head – required a well-defined waist, a short, compact and sturdy body; indeed, when picking up a pekingese it should be unexpectedly compact and heavy, rather like picking up a faggot or billet of wood. The front legs had to be shorter than the hind legs, with the object of producing a rolling gait, the movement of 'a plentifully finned goldfish'. The forelegs were to be short, not straight and stick-like. This last point has led to endless controversy among Western breeders, as some of the Chinese paintings undoubtedly show pekingese with straight legs, but, if one goes back to the lion, the legs should be, as Collier lays down, turned slightly outwards at the shoulder and there must be a slight curvature thence down to the toes which, too, should turn outwards, but not enough to produce the serious defect called 'crab-toes'.

Western requirements differ slightly from these except that the 'apple' or dome head has disappeared, but from ancient China to our century there has always been the question of size; in 1908 the Pekingese Club split into adherents of the Club and a new Pekin Palace Dog Association which said the breed was getting coarse and too large and limited the weight to ten pounds, saying toy dogs should be small. (The British Kennel Club now lays down 7–10 pounds for male pekingese, 8–11 for bitches, for easier breeding, and a separate class for the miniature under 6 pounds.)

This harks back to the 'Sleeve Dog', a name still obstinately used by people today. 'The smaller the more treasured' as Dr Caius had remarked and the demand reached its peak in the Tao-kuang period, 1821–1850, when a reliable Chinese wrote:

> A breed recognised as sleeve-dogs exists at Aigun in Hai-Lung-Kiang, and in all the vicinity. I have a friend who is a native of I-lan, where, he says, sleeve-dogs are very plentiful. They are very small and extremely intelligent. They can take things with their mouths as men do with their hands. They know how to sit, beg, roll and do other tricks. . . .
>
> Most of the rich persons, managers of shops, or those of such inclination keep these dogs. During the period when big sleeves were fashionable, these dogs were kept in the sleeves and were called 'sleeve-dogs'.

But broad sleeves were out of fashion in China from 1900 onwards and the Empress Tzŭ-hsi had a horror of the artificial dwarfing of the dogs; some methods were abominably cruel: the puppies were put into wire cages that closely fitted their bodies and which were only taken off when they were mature –

a practice as torturing as the foot-binding of little Chinese girls. It has had its effect on the breed because, as we have seen, pekingese do not breed 'true'; also, only a few of the miniature dogs are truly robust and have 'that fearless carriage' of the typical pekingese. Even when they are strong and hardy, often foolhardy, being so small they are frighteningly vulnerable; one can so easily tread on them and, absolutely fearless, they will bounce up to a big dog who might mistake them for a rabbit — one shake and the neck is broken. My own Cumquat was crushed to death when the postman shut our heavy front door on her; it was her fault, not the postman's, as she always tried to dart outside. These tiny pekingese are so quick that they seem not to run but skim the ground; to have a truly good one is like owning a sturdy independent butterfly — but they are irresistible.

Dogs playing

All the first five brought back to England were small. Lord John Hay's dog Schlorff, a rich chestnut with a dark mask, weighed four and a half pounds, but he was evidently hardy as he lived for another eighteen years with Lord John and must have approached the record in pekingese for longevity, twenty-five years. The bitch, a little black and white called Hytien, Lord John gave to his sister, the Duchess of Wellington, who began the breed at Stratfield Saye.

Sir George Fitzroy's two, also small and, like Schlorff, dark chestnut, black masked, went to his cousin, the Duchess of Richmond and Gordon. The dog was Guli and the bitch may have been the first Meh, and from them, perhaps with the help of Schlorff and a few later importations, evolved the Good-wood strain carried on by Lady Algernon Gordon-Lennox and which contributed to so many famous kennels.

When one looks at photographs of these early importations, and the few that followed them up to the turn of the century, and compares them with the painting and scrolls of dogs in China at that time, it can be seen that they were not good specimens; it is unlikely that the Court, when it retreated to Jehol, hastily but in all its panoply, would have left its valuable ones behind. On the Court's return, as the pekingese were still guarded in the Palace, the dogs remained rare. Even with the new trading concessions forced on the Chinese, the establishment of what they had dreaded, foreign legations in Peking itself, and considering the busy comings and goings between China and the outside world – and the fact that there were no laws of quarantine in those days – it is astonishing that during the forty years after the burning of the Summer Palace only a trickle of genuine pekingese were brought to Europe, which seems to discountenance the stories, still told in the families of those first officers, of 'hundreds of little dogs running about

Lord John Hay and Schlorff in the 1860s

abandoned in the palace', and of the Chaplain Thelwall's 'so many they were taken away in carts', because where did they go? I think these families are thinking of the Boxer rebellion of 1900 when the Empress and her attendants fled in such disorder that there was no time to gather up more than an armful of dogs.

Even most Chinese had never seen one which is shown by the sad tale of Little Apricot, a miniature that in the late 1890s Mrs Archibald Little took up-country.

> . . . the people gathered round him, calling him 'Little Lion', 'Little Sleeve dog', 'Cat dog', and asked leave to stroke him. 'He comes from Peking', they said with pride and pleasure.

Little Apricot only lived a year and his story, told in *Intimate China*, is the first account written in English of a pekingese.

Sir Chalmer Alabaster, who was Consul General in Canton, said that in thirty years of living in China, he had never seen one in Canton and only as a great rarity in Peking, and another resident wrote that it was only after 'five years of endeavour' that he succeeded in getting a pair.

Mrs Loftus Allen, who went to China in 1891 determined to find one, failed in spite of ceaseless enquiries and searchings. Her husband, in command of a merchant ship visiting Shanghai, succeeded in buying a grey-brindle pekingese from a taxidermist – was the taxidermist going to stuff it? He swore it came from the Imperial palace and Captain Loftus Allen was sure it had been stolen particularly when it was explained that the sale must be kept secret and the dog only delivered on board when the ship was ready to sail. This dog was Pekin Peter whom, in her ignorance, Mrs Loftus Allen advertised for stud as 'a rough-coated pekingese pug'. Captain Loftus Allen had a friend in Shanghai whose groom's brother was an eunuch in the palace. Through him two more pekingese were acquired – once again stolen. They were Pekin Prince and Pekin Princess.

So, in ones and twos, but generally in pairs, between 1861 and 1900, the pekingese appeared, slowly but steadily, bobbing up in unexpected places. Some were certainly gifts but in 1896, the same year as the arrival of the Pekin Prince and Princess, another pair were, according to their owners, Mr and Mrs Douglas Murray, smuggled out of the palace hidden in a hay-box inside a crate containing Japanese deer. These were Ah Cum and Mimosa. Still, none of these seem to have been really good specimens and it is something of a miracle that they developed into the exquisite race we know today, far better than anything seen in China. I often wonder what the Empress Tzŭ-hsi or her father-in-law, the Emperor Tao-kuang, an even greater connoisseur, would have said if they could have seen some of the great swanks of the Western show ring, or even our ordinary 'home' or domestic pekingese.

How little the English importers of those early days knew of one another is shown by an encounter between the Douglas Murrays and Lady Algernon Gordon-Lennox. One day in London Lady Algernon caught a passing glimpse of the Douglas Murrays walking Ah Cum and Mimosa and she chased them down the street; both sides were equally astonished to find the other owned similar dogs and to them belongs the honour of producing between them the first English champion, Goodwood Lo. The next was also a Goodwood, Champion Goodwood Chun, whose mahogany red coat so impressed Dr Vlasto.

There was a decline in the last two decades of the nineteenth century because of lack of good out-cross dogs, but in 1900 came an important stud force, Glanbrane Boxer, given to Major J. H. Gwynne of the 23rd Welsh Fusiliers by Prince Ch'ing in return for special services during the chaos of the Boxer Rebellion in Peking. Prince Ch'ing was a high official of the Imperial Court, so these two – there was a bitch as well – were indisputably palace dogs. Boxer was a great influence on the breed because he had the flat skull, the 'abacus head' of the Chinese, which helped to eradicate the 'dome-shaped' which had become despised.

Though Boxer became a famous sire, he was never shown because he had a docked tail. Tails were occasionally docked in China, arising perhaps from the first attempts to make the pet dogs look like a lion dog by shaving the tail and leaving a tuft at the end. Princess Der-ling wrote that the Empress told her that the ends of the tails were bitten off when the puppies were ten days old to make the tails more feathery, but the

Princess is not wholly to be relied on. A still uglier story is that the Empress Tzŭ-hsi docked the tails of any dogs she bestowed as gifts from the palace stud which is contradicted by the fact that in her last years she gave some beautiful dogs away, for instance, to Miss Carl, but she did have them neutered to prevent their breeding. The Empress, by nature, was jealous; Miss Carl had seen that she did not like her dogs to give attention to anyone but herself, so the artist was careful not to take notice of, or pet them, but,

> Among the younger set . . . was one that caught my fancy – he was a beautiful white and amber coloured pekingese pug [sic]. He soon learned to know me and would come running to me. One night, when we had finished dinner at Her Majesty's table, one of her eunuchs brought in this very little dog and put it into my arms saying that Her Majesty had presented him to me.

It seems that the Empress's spies had told of those secret afternoon visits to the dogs' courtyard. She told Miss Carl that the dog should be named Me-lah-Golden Amber. After this he never left Miss Carl's side, becoming her constant companion and faithful friend. She took him back to America – one of the first pekingese to arrive there, though a Mr Harry Kendall brought two from Manchuria in 1900, three or four years before Me-lah arrived.

Miss Carl was evidently a good woman as well as a good artist; aware that any account of her experience in the palaces would be looked on by the Chinese as a breach of etiquette – any comment favourable or unfavourable on the 'sacred persons' of the Emperor or Empress was breaking the rule of

Chinese propriety – she was driven to write only by the slanders and scandals about the Empress Tzŭ-hsi in the British and American press. No such loyalty or consideration seem to have bothered the Chinese Princess Der-ling, but it is through her more fanciful and, as has been seen, critical books, that one learns most about the Empress and her deep interest in, and knowledge of, her dogs.

> On the day of Black Jade's puppies, when the morning Audience was over and Her Majesty had changed to less formal attire for walking, we went around Thousand Years Hill to the kennels . . . Her Majesty called my attention to one dog that was tendered her, one of the four puppies.
>
> 'See this one?' she said. 'It is the best of the four. Its markings are perfect. Its mother is Black Jade', she indicated a coal-black female in a cage, 'and its father is Black-Cloud-over-Snow', she indicated another dog, the male, which was dead black, a perfect animal, except for the legs, which were snow white. It was easy to see the derivation of the animal's name. 'These other three are poorly marked. This one's hind legs are not enough longer than its front ones. This one's body is a trifle too long. This one's tail will curl backward instead of forward'. So she banished three of Black Jade's beautiful puppies.

What of the rejects, those banished ones? Some tales say they were killed, others that the eunuchs took them and sold them in spite of the punishment if smuggling were found out. Dr Rennie, in his book, avers that a fair was held for six days every month at the Lung Fu Ssu Temple in Peking and there it

Screen painted by Maud Earl, who made many pekingese portraits in Edwardian days

was possible to buy pekingese from the eunuchs who dared to sell inferior or discarded ones. Certainly up to the time of the Boxer rebellion, those pekingese that came to the West were not of the finest quality.

There is an English quip about pekingese in which there are 'peer pekes', then 'vere pekes' – beautifully bred but not in championship class: 'mere pekes', and 'near pekes' – those that have been unfortunately crossed – but all are 'dear pekes'.

The Empress Tzŭ-hsi would not have agreed but I must

confess that one of my most 'dear', even dearest of all, was exceedingly 'mere'. It had not taken long for me to become a true pekingese snob so that I would never have had the wit to buy him but, in Calcutta, took him and his father out of pity for a friend who had to go back to England and leave her dogs behind. I shall not forget the day she left them with me; both pekingese went to the end of the lawn and sat with their backs to the house, their heads turned resolutely away to the wall. They did not die, as did the dogs bereft in Chinese history, as my own white bitch Moon Daisy died in six weeks when, in my turn, I was forced to leave her in India; they lived, perhaps because I did not attempt to cajole them but respected their grief.

I say lived, but the father, Sol, rather, consented to stay with us – on his terms. In those days of many servants in India, the lowest was the sweeper, an 'untouchable', whose duty was to keep the house floors clean, attend to the bath-rooms – and the dogs. Our Untouchable was a magnificent man called Khokil who looked as if he would breed sons. He was a tall well-made man like a Rajput, the fighting race, strong and impressive with big features and a big moustache, more like a general than a sweeper. He wore good clothes, a spotless flowing dhoti, a khaki shirt and a black silk hat, and had manners and courtesy.

He was with our family for years and shared my passion for pekingese. On feast days Khokil gave each dog a chupatti, a soft biscuit like a waffle, that he bought in the bazaar. Every dog he looked after, every puppy, remembered and adored him, but Sol would never allow Khokil to brush, walk or even feed him. If Sol were ever scolded he would walk out of the house to his original stance, back turned at the end of the lawn until I begged his pardon. He lived to be fourteen and would have gone on longer but he got rabies, that scourge of India. This

was a death I could not bring myself to describe when I wrote
of Sol in *Rungli-Rungliot* or *Thus Far and no Further*, an account of
a winter spent on a tea-garden. In it I gave him the death I
would have chosen for him, when he simply rolled over in the
sun and was gone.

Sol was a mandarin, golden-coated, but his son, Wing!
Pekingese do not breed well in India, as I had learned, but
never have I seen such a disgrace to the race as Wing. To begin
with he was truly liver-coloured, smooth-coated, not a trace
of feathering and had a ruff of such peculiar coarseness that it
stuck out like a collar of quills. His tail was a tuft, his legs
bowed almost to a half-hoop – I am sure he had 'crab toes';
his nose was brown – unthinkable – and his face had the
hideousness of a cheerful kylin, but even in a thousand years
there could never have been another Wing; he did not know
of course how hideous he was nor, soon, did I, nor even that
super-snob, far worse than I, Khokil.

It was partly Wing's cleverness, his spirit of fun; recounting
tricks of one's dogs is boring, so I will refrain, but must say I
have not known another that would play hide-and-seek with
people, hiding himself and springing out to take them by surprise. It was partly, too, his philosophy: when he first came he
was mortally afraid of water and would never swim in the
'tanks' or pools as, in the hot weather, the other pekingese did,
but one year we went to the Coromandel coast where the huge
surf-rollers pound along the beach; bathers there have to wear
the local fishermen's pointed wicker helmets to break the wave
and prevent themselves from being stunned. One evening we
were walking on the sand by moonlight and Wing was catching
crabs and followed them too far downshore; in a moment a
roller caught him and swept him far out into the Indian Ocean.
We thought he was gone for ever but the next wave brought
him back, rolling him stunned, bruised, breathless and sodden

at our feet. Most dogs would have dreaded water even more
after that, but Wing was never afraid again.

He came to Kashmir and was with us on the long treks we
made in the Himalayas, over passes sometimes up to 17,000
feet. Others of the pekingese have trekked with me too – perhaps on twenty-mile marches; some of the time they rode on
top of the packs of the pack ponies, but not Wing – if I
walked, he walked, even when his pads grew sore from glacier
ice and rough stones.

When we made camp he would sit by our cook-guide as, in
the marvellous way these men have, Subhan conjured up a
cook-fire, kindled between stones. Subhan always cooked
Wing's supper first. After it one would have thought a small
dog would be tired but no – he would ask for his walnut: a
ball would have bounced down the mountain, so Wing made
do with a walnut which travelled in Subhan's saddlebag; he
would play with it with as much zest as he did with his ball at
home.

All my pekingese were dear to me yet with only four – perhaps with Jade Button there will be five – did the dearness go
deep into the cockles of my heart, if a heart has cockles. Wing
was perhaps closest of all but, of all my pekingese, he met the
worst end.

In Kashmir the vale becomes, in summer, intolerably hot;
even the lakes, with the beauty of their lotus in full flower,
seem stagnant, while the canals of Srinagar reek. We lived
outside the city but still, every July, we left for the mountains
and camped for three months in Sonamarg which means
literally 'meadow of gold'. It was high, 9,000 feet, and our
chosen site, rented from the – in those days – State of Kashmir,
was on the edge of the forest and, of course, by a stream. The
cook-tent and servants' tents were behind; then came a living-
dining tent with a rough-hewn floor – it often rained – beside

it two bedroom tents in which my sister and I slept, each with a child and, below us, a smaller tent for my eldest girl and her nurse. The dogs slept in baskets, their leashes tied to the centre tent pole and a lantern was left burning at the entrance of each tent because we knew that lynx and foxes were about; we had not dreamed of anything else.

Nana was Italian-Swiss with a Swiss passion for hygiene but, even at that altitude, as the days grew warmer we were beset by fleas. They came only from the grass but every night when Nana had gone to bed we would hear screams, 'Madre! Mama Mama mia!' and the sound of pillows beaten, blankets shaken. Nana had found a flea. We turned over and went to sleep.

One night, at about half past ten, the screams were louder but again none of us took any notice until they went on and on then seemed to grow fainter as if Nana were outside. I sprang out of bed as did my sister and the head pony man.

Indeed Nana was outside; something large had leaped into the tent and seized Wing from his basket. Nana, in her night-gown and bare feet, had given chase – she had no idea what had taken Wing. Her screams, her apparition in a white night-gown, frightened the creature into dropping him.

It was a snow leopard; the Chinese say dog flesh is the wine of leopards, but to leap past a lantern into a tent that held humans was unknown.

We laid Wing on a table while my sister took the blood-stained and shaking Nana away. Wing was alive but the claws had slashed his stomach; already it was distending and, in his mutilated little clown face, his eyes staring with horror were beyond any comprehending. Even Sol, in the intervals between the convulsions of rabies, had been able to hear my voice, feel my hands, but with Wing all was blotted out.

He died ten minutes later.

CHAPTER SIX

The Alderbournes

ALDERBOURNE PEKINGESE, brother and sister, three
months old, red, black mask, beauties, £75 and £80.
ALDERBOURNE PEKINGESE, exquisite, pure white bitch
ready now, £150.
ALDERBOURNE PEKINGESE, three litters, just ready,
show specimens.
ALDERBOURNE PEKINGESE, pure black miniature.

These advertisements appeared in the London *Times*
every Friday. Now and again to some advertisement
and almost as an afterthought would be added,
'Puppies from twenty-five guineas'. Until recently it was
possible to buy a pedigreed pekingese for that price, though it
was usually forty or fifty guineas; if the price were not mentioned it was sure to be high and, of course, the real 'show
specimens' were not advertised; there were always breeders and
special clients all over the world waiting for those.

The Alderbourne ranks as the oldest and certainly the best known kennel of pekingese in any country. No other, so far, has equalled its record. As Ellic Howe said, 'It's quite simple. If one wanted to buy the best car in the world one would buy a Rolls Royce; if one wanted the best pekingese one would buy an Alderbourne'. This is not to say there are not other kennels of equal standard, for instance the Cavershams, but it is impossible to write of them all and I have chosen Alderbourne, not simply for its record but because it is the kennel I know best and from which, during forty years of friendship, almost all my pekingese have come.

It began, or was conceived, in 1904, from the moment when Mrs Ashton Cross saw a strange looking little animal being carried in Piccadilly. Intrigued by its oddness, she asked what it was and, on being told it came from China and was a pekingese, determined she must have one. When Mrs Ashton Cross 'determined' anything it happened and soon she had bought a little bitch from a Mrs MacEwen, the artist Millais's daughter. It was named Manchu Tzŭ which, had they known it, was incredible impertinence.

Clarice Ashton Cross was a well known beauty, married to an equally well known and rich barrister; they had two sons and four daughters, all under her sway because she was as imperious as she was beautiful, knew exactly what she wanted and had the integrity to hold to that vision, supporting it with an uncommonly skilled understanding of animals – in 1904 she already had an Arab horse stud and a kennel of bloodhounds. The pekingese soon ousted them.

That first imperially named little bitch was in whelp so that the Ashton Cross daughters, the Misses Aimée, Violette, Marjorie and Cynthia, each hoped for a pet of her own, but only one puppy was born and that had to go to Mrs McEwen as part of the stud price. Four other bitches were bought, 'To keep the peace', as Miss Cynthia tells, but soon professionalism, an innate quality, took charge and Mrs Ashton Cross decided to buy the best possible of these rare puppies, to found a kennel and breed and, so, in 1904, bought a dog puppy, three months old. Her husband, rich as he was, almost collapsed when he heard the price, but Mrs Ashton Cross had an 'eye'; the puppy was Champion Chu-êrh of Alderbourne who became not only the founder of the kennel but the chief influence of the breed and perhaps the most famous – certainly the most highly priced – pekingese who ever lived.

The earlier Ah Cum (1896), one of the two dogs supposedly smuggled out of the Palace in the cage of Japanese deer was, though he only lived ten years, undoubtedly head of the genealogical tree of pekingese in the West, as can be seen from Ch. Chu-êrh's pedigree where his name appears four times. Out of Lady Algernon Gordon-Lennox's Goodwood Meh, Ah Cum begot Goodwood Lo, the first pekingese champion and from Ah Cum and the Goodwoods, Lo and Chun, came the three main branches from which all our best pekingese descend: the Alderbournes founded on Ch. Chu-êrh, the Sutherlands descended from Ouen Teu T'ang, and the Broadoaks from the black and tan Broadoak Beetle; all born in the same year.

Champion Chu-êrh of Alderbourne with his cups

These lines prevailed, not only in Britain where kennels of note – and some indifferent ones – proliferated but also in the rest of Europe, and in America, Canada, Australia, India; Britain though was in the lead; indeed, as early as 1913 it was easier to buy a first-rate pekingese in London than in Peking and, ironically, by 1921 the Chinese were importing pekingese from England.

Most influential of the three was Ch. Chu-êrh. He and Ouen Teu T'ang were litter brothers – what a litter! but Chu-êrh outshone even his famous brother, just as he surpassed Broadoak Beetle.

The Beetle line, so important from 1914–1939, dwindled out; after 1945 it yielded only one champion descended in tail-male (13 generations). Likewise, after 1945, only one champion came from the line of Sutherland Ouen Teu T'ang while Ch. Chu-êrh sired fifteen champions and, in those days, championships for pekingese were few and far between; Chuty, his son, the remarkable red and white parti-colour, born in 1909, even surpassed him as almost all the post-1914 war champions were descended tail-male from him, while Ch. Chu-êrh's grandson Ch. Choo-Tai became Champion of All Breeds at Crufts Show – until recently the only 'toy' dog who has won it – a record he held for sixty years. Their descendants include, in the Alderbourne kennel or sired by its dogs, two hundred and fifty champions; in fact the kennel, in seventy years of existence, against fierce competition, has won more than two hundred and sixty thousand prizes – and this is a conservative estimate.

Looking from Ah Cum himself as he stands, disturbingly lifelike, in the Zoological Museum at Tring, to the Alderbournes and their kindred kennels of today, one can see how wonderfully the breed has improved.

Ah Cum, 'disturbingly lifelike'

Ah Cum, beautiful in colour and carriage, is light-boned with straight forelegs, his coat comparatively light, his tail more like a tuft than a plume, while Ch. Chu-êrh's stamp is on the Alderbournes even now. Besides his style and showmanship, he had a strong well-shaped body, short legs correctly bowed, a red coat fully feathered and a perfect fall of tail.

He was too as brave and sporting as any pekingese – too brave and too sporting. One afternoon Miss Cynthia looked out of her window and saw the Arab mares and foals running in panic. It was Chu-êrh, then three years old, chasing them. Then one of the mares kicked him and he rolled over; all three watchers thought in terror that this must be the end of Chu-êrh but after a moment he picked himself up, shook out his coat and went on chasing. Another time, he and his companions put thirty or more bloodhounds to flight, the big hounds running for dear life, chased by the triumphant pekingese.

The Alderbourne kennel was built up by careful line breeding from Chu-êrh and, from his sons – Chuty and his brothers Wong-ti, Chu-êrh Tu – and from Choo-Tai – came four more lines which Mrs Ashton Cross was careful to keep distinct. These dogs were mated with bitches of varying pedigree, then their 'children' were mated together, line breeding back to Chu-êrh. From time to time fresh blood was brought in but this often resulted in faults; in fact, the best results were achieved by mating half-brother to half-sister, and grandson to grand-daughter, some of the same blood being allowed on both sides. In-breeding, though, was never overdone as the ideal was, first of all, soundness. Next came intelligence – a heavy skull with plenty of brain room, then balance, an abundant coat but not overdone – 'Some of the overbred dogs of today look as if they were drowning in hair', says Miss Cynthia – then pride in tail and carriage; with it the characteristic fearlessness and, always, handsomeness in colouring and, especially, in the beautiful dark eyes known the world over as Alderbourne eyes.

Of course, only a few, very few, among the myriad Alderbourne puppies were of top standard; most were sold as house pets, companions, but even a little of the Alderbourne blood can give a look of style, as if these lesser ones knew that the names of their great relations make a litany in pekingese history: Champion Yu Tong, Ch. Tong-Tu, Ch. Ling Yu Fang – grandfather, father and son. Miss Cynthia's own favourite, the proud Ch. Tulyar and his son Ch. Tul Tao; Ch. Meng; Ch. Chuanne; Ch. Choo Tai – of outstanding intelligence; the exquisite bitch Ch. Yula; Ch. China Doll whom the Ashton Crosses consider the best bitch ever bred – her son Chinaman and his nephew Princely Gift became renowned. Then there were the miniatures: Chick – perhaps the perkiest of them all – Ch. Bumble Bee and, my favourite of all time, Ch. Humming Bee. His son Beeswing, though so small, could hurdle like Tai-Tu and sit up and beg on his mistress's hand; Humming Bee, equally small, thought that beneath his dignity.

The great days of the kennel are now over; Miss Cynthia, the last Miss Ashton Cross, was born in 1895 and can no longer go to shows or run a big kennel – it is, in fact, almost private – but not a week passes without a telephone call, from overseas as well as Britain, asking for a puppy, and there is a steady flow of letters. The kennel, though, still has the famous pure white Limelight of Alderbourne, father of my own Radiant Light – known in this family as Ton-Ton.

The highest price offered for any dog of any breed was offered for Ch. Chu-êrh by Mr Pierpont Morgan. The first price was £10,000, then it rose to £25,000, then £32,000 and, when that was refused, he offered a blank cheque. It was refused too and the newspapers ran a story that there were three things in England even Pierpont Morgan could not buy: good weather, a British policeman and Mrs Ashton Cross's dog.

That was the whim of a multi-millionaire but, even among less ostentatious people, prices for pekingese in Edwardian times were extraordinarily high; in the early 1900s Lord Decies paid £3,000 for four or five dogs while offers up to four thousand dollars from America for one puppy were often refused; it is the integrity and courage of such refusals that gives a kennel its quality – that and hard work. At its peak, there were more than two hundred dogs in the Alderbourne kennels; those that were not personal pets were kept in airy bungalows with sixty-foot runs where they could scamper and play as the Imperial dogs played in the palace courtyards at Peking. They had a hurdling race course for exercise – and fun – and, with

Champion Tai-Tu of Alderbourne, hurdling

six kennel-maids in attendance as well as the devoted daughters to tend them, were never left alone for long. There were separate 'nurseries' for the puppies.

The hardest work was the keeping of the records: show winnings; stud records; whelping records; sales; transfers; registrations; deaths and, of course, births. Ellic Howe tried to compile the pedigree of his Yula of Redstock back to Chu-êrh, fifteen generations, and Ah Cum, nineteen, and gave it up in despair when he realised that the complete document would require over 1,048,574 names! It was indeed hard work; try writing 'Ch. Alderbourne China Doll of Kaytocli' in a two-inch space. All champion names had to be written in red ink which meant changing pens and all entries had to be checked; it took endless patience – as did the shows.

Leading up to every show were long hours of grooming and training; to groom an everyday pekingese, if there is such a thing, takes up to half an hour; for a show dog that might be doubled. Then the dog or bitch has to be trained to stand and to 'show'. For a few years Alderbournes were entered for the Obedience Classes at Cruft's and won them – even with the minute Beeswing. He was outstandingly clever and could do everything the big dogs did – fetch dumb bells, sit, come when called, hurdle and jump, though the jumps were commensurate with his size. Tai-Tu, whose photograph hurdling appeared in almost every newspaper in the world, once came down nine feet from his take-off. He weighed just eleven pounds.

Perhaps the hardest test required that the dog should be brought into the ring hungry and, when given a plate of his favourite food, sit by it until he was told to eat; the time was four minutes and the owner had to go out of sight, leaving the dog alone with his tempting plate. Hundreds of people were watching when, on one occasion, Beeswing and his plate came into the ring. He was ravenous and the four minutes must have seemed interminable; he endured for two and then, without moving from his post, slowly got up and, in Miss Cynthia's words, 'sat on his bottom and begged'. The crowd roared but he did not move a muscle. He had not broken the rules but instead of sitting on four legs sat on two; after another two minutes the judge called her; Beeswing saw his mistress come into the ring but knew he still must not move as she walked up and stood beside him. She had to wait for the word from the judge. It came, she released Beeswing who literally jumped on the food and gobbled it. To claps and cheers the tiny dog won, but the Ashton Crosses were asked not to enter pekingese for Obedience Classes again as they made the big dogs look absurd.

Pekingese are notoriously wilful and to train them to such obedience is an extraordinary feat. No wonder the two younger Miss Ashton Crosses became international judges: the eldest was fatally injured in an accident, the second daughter became crippled, but Miss Marjorie and Miss Cynthia went on to judge in Paris, Geneva and Milan. They accompanied their

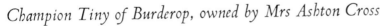

Champion Tiny of Burderop, owned by Mrs Ashton Cross

This page
International champion
Alderbourne Lifu of
Remward (now in
America)

Alderbourne Rhapsody
in Blue (see page 135)

Australian Champion
Princely Light of
Alderbourne

Right: Champion Ho
Dynasty's Ballad, bred
by Joanne Goble in Mary-
land, and American
and Bermudian Cham-
pion

The smallest pekingese
ever bred at Alderbourne
— it weighed $2\frac{1}{2}$ lbs at
eight months

Three generations of
champions: Ch. Chu-êrh
and Ch. Chuty of
Alderbourne and Ch.
Choo-Tai of Egham

dogs, too, when they were bought for overseas, travelling to America, India and Egypt. Alderbournes have gone to countries as far apart as Australia and Alaska; cables announcing their triumphs fill albums in the kennel records.

When, recently, I went to see Miss Cynthia at Ascot, across the hall table lay a band of ribbons: 'Best Pekingese Puppy', 'Best of Breed', 'Best in Group', 'Best toy puppy in Show'. They came from Australia where a young Alderbourne dog had gone at four months old; he spent three months in quarantine and emerged to go straight to a show and win those ribbons.

In the Edwardian years it seems shows were like garden parties, gentlemanly affairs; the Ashton Crosses used to arrive in carriages with footmen to carry the hampers of dogs and hampers of food and serve luncheon and tea.

It was also what one can only call the 'silly' time of pekingese – the years from late Edwardian to post-war Georgian, perhaps even up to the thirties, seem tinctured through and

'Pagoda Winky'; an example of twentieth-century 'chinoiserie'

through with artificiality, hypocrisy and silliness. The pekingese world was no exception; there were charity dog shows
where the dogs were dressed in clothes and treated as live dolls;
books that purported to be written by pekingese – I was guilty
of one; it was in fact the first book I had published and at
least it had, even in those days, some genuine Chinese research;
it got excellent reviews but now I blush for it. Chinoiserie had
at least been elegant; this was embarrassingly 'precious' and did
the breed no good. There was the cult of the Pearls and E. V.
Lucas produced his Pekinese National Anthem:

The Pekinese
Disdain to please
   On any set design,
But make a thrall
Of one and all
   By simple Right Divine.

*   *   *   *

The Pekinese
Demosthenes
   Requires no voice to plead:
Those shining eyes,
So soft, so wise,
   Get everything they need.

The Pekinese
Abstain from fleas
   And doggy things like that,

But hate it when
Unthinking men
   Compare them to the cat.

The Pekinese
From Autumn trees
   Their colour scheme obtain;
And all their lives
Their frugal wives
   From any change refrain.

The Pekinese
Have feathered knees,
   And plumes where tails should be,
And as they race
About the place
   They ripple like the sea.

        *   *   *   *

The Pekinese
Adore their ease
   And slumber like the dead;
In comfort curled
They view the world
   As one unending bed.

The Pekinese
On China's seas
   Embarked to win the West;
A piece of Ming
's a lovely thing,
   But oh! the dogs are best.

E. V. Lucas sent it to Mrs Ashton Cross decorated with hand-painted pekingese but sadly the copy has been lost, sadly because, though undoubted whimsy, pekingese-wise it is completely truthful; and, in those early shows, though sometimes they seem amateur, there was a refreshing friendliness between the rival kennels; those great breeders even showed dogs for one another with a generosity seldom seen today. Even in the nineteen-forties Miss Cynthia flew in a private plane to a north of England show, taking Ch. Ku-Chi of Caversham, son of the famous Puff Ball of Chunking, and was delighted to bring him home to his owner with the Championship though she had also entered three dogs of her own. 'It was a great honour to take him', she said. 'He was a very great champion'.

Dog shows, though, soon became cut-throat affairs often based, not on love of a breed, but pure commercialism; a win at Cruft's can increase a dog's value, indeed the value of its whole breed a hundred-fold – and put it in jeopardy. There were several attempts to kill Ch. Chu-êrh; once when Miss Violette had him in her arms a man came up to stroke him and, just in time, she saw he had a needled syringe hidden in his hand; she managed to strike his hand down and he disappeared in the crowd. No dog could be left alone for a second – in fact, sometimes one was guarded by a policeman – yet there was a tragedy with one of the later champions, Choo Tai. At a Southampton show Miss Cynthia took him with her to luncheon and, on coming back, put him in his cage. There were some grains of coffee sugar in his saucer but as it was an Ashton Cross habit to show with sugar as a reward she thought nothing of it. He had won the Open Class and had to go in for the Championship but, when she lifted him out of the cage, to her surprise he did not seem well. She hesitated, but he had the typical pekingese courage, went into the ring and showed perfectly, winning the Championship and Best of Breed. Then he collapsed and, in spite of every effort to save him, died. The sugar put into his saucer was strychnine.

It seems wrong to build up a dog to such a height that he is exposed to these devilish risks but a few dogs, like a few people, are born actors, natural show-offs, and happiest in the ring.

There is too a deep satisfaction in breeding an exquisite animal. I have known it in a far humbler way when my white Moon Daisy was mated to an equally white dog newly imported into India. He belonged to an Armenian lady as proud as himself and reputed to be an expert on pekingese; the fee was large and included the pick of the litter.

Moon had four white puppies; the first, a bitch, was large but arrived early; the next two, both bitches, were more difficult; the last, the only male, a real struggle; as I took him out in my hand, I had never seen a puppy so small.

Pekingese, newborn, look like minuscule seals, especially when still wet; this, most minuscule of all, was strong, breathing steadily and soon it became clear that we had a small, beautifully formed miniature, pure white with great dark eyes. Indians came in crowds to see him, especially Buddhists, as was fitting, because the country Buddhists say that a white animal, any white animal, is a beautiful soul upon its path up the Ladder of Existence, so fine a soul that it will one day be the Buddha, and so they came to reverence this tiny white dog. 'But don't set your heart on him', I warned Khokil. 'The Mem is bound to take him'.

Khokil did not answer but his moustaches quivered.

In choosing the pick of the litter, the stud dog owner has to make the choice by the time the puppies are two months old. By then the first born was a snowball of fluff, takingly pretty but showing a tendency to light bone – always the danger when breeding in India; the dog puppy, not half her size, was heavier than she, large skulled, flat-faced, but the day came and, 'Khokil', I said, 'you will not touch the dog puppy nor do anything to him. You understand?'

Khokil did not answer.

I took the Armenian Mem out on the verandah where the puppies were gambolling in a playpen – all but one. In the corner of the pen lay a tiny dejected listless object, the eyes tight shut and, most surprisingly of all, its coat a brownish cream. 'Khokil! What . . .' I began. Khokil looked into the air.

'You will of course want the miniature dog', I told the lady.

'That!' She glared. 'What a little misery. It will not live and do you think I don't know quality when I see it?' and she picked up the fluffy bitch.

'But . . . she's too light. That prettiness won't last . . . while he . . .' In the face of her scorn I felt I was babbling.

'He is not even white and I specified white.'

There was nothing more I could say – except to Khokil.

'I did not touch him . . . just as you said. Is it *my* fault', Khokil demanded, 'if the little badmash – bad one – stepped into a saucer of coffee and spilled it all over him?'

The puppy grew to be Candytuft – a perfect miniature with a coat of spun white, setting off his dark eyes – only he burned part of his tail off in a camp fire and broke his jaw in a fight with a Tibetan mastiff. He was so small that when he was mated he had to stand on a dictionary, yet he was one of the four pekingese I took up the Zoji La Pass into Little Tibet and up the Nichnai Pass, 13,000 feet.

Even 'Untouchables' like Khokil have their distinctions and he could not touch anything dead because then it had become carrion. If a crow fell dead in our garden Khokil had to fetch a boy of even lower caste to pick it up and carry it away – it always touched me that the boy, who usually went naked, put on a shirt to do this ritual task – but the day Candytuft died Khokil himself took up the little body and buried it with his own hands.

*   *   *   *

Queen Victoria disliked dog shows though she was besieged by requests to show her rare animals and, after an epidemic of distemper ravaged the Windsor kennels, she refused to allow any of hers to be shown again. Such an idea never entered the Empress Tzŭ-hsi's mind. She kept her dogs for pleasure and relief and no one perhaps has better understood the necessity of these two qualities than she.

One day the Viceroy of Canton, a nobleman she had trusted and loved, was impeached for dishonesty, cruelty and de-bauchery. She had to order that he 'strip the coral button of rank from his cap, tear away the peacock feather, that his lands, property and money be confiscated and that he be exiled' – which meant that neither he nor his descendants could hold office again; the loss of face was more tragic than decapitation and the day was filled with gloom with the Empress deeply de-pressed. Suddenly her face brightened. 'Tomorrow the lotus buds will be opening', she said, and gave the order for the whole court to rise before dawn and go out on the lake.

Princess Der-ling described that moment of solace and wonder:

> Her Majesty sat on a throne raised above the rest of the boat, where the court ladies were permitted to sit down. The barge was pushed by poles to where lotus pads covered the surface of the water with a carpet of green. Her Majesty spoke softly.

'Stop the barge. Wait, watch, and listen!'

. . . off to the east the sun had not yet risen, though the sky was beginning to be faintly tinged with red . . . birds, their voices muted as though they felt the early morning spell, flew low over us, their wings stirring the cool air. Ahead of us the lotus pads moved back and forth on the water . . . the face of Her Majesty was placid – for she knew what was to transpire. She seemed . . . wrapped in her thoughts. . . .

'Watch', she said softly, 'the buds will open when the sun comes up'. . . . There was no doubt that she had forgotten the Viceroy of Canton. Her whole soul was intent on the rising sun, and the fat buds of the lotus.

Now we could see the top of the red disc of the sun, and now even Her Majesty spoke in a whisper.

'Watch!' she said.

All eyes were fastened intently now on the bed of lotus . . . for the buds were moving. Hundreds of them, thousands of them, as far on either hand as the eye could reach. . . .

The sun lifted higher.

Bigger grew the buds of the lotus.

And as the sun lifted and the buds spread, the delicate odour of the lotus flowed out upon us, and over us, as the dawn itself swept over us out of the east . . ..

I caught myself listening, as all the bed of lotus stirred, because by some trick of vision, I thought I could hear the opening of the buds.

Stronger grew the perfume.

Birds flew over swiftly with only the sound of softly whirring wings. . . . Brighter and brighter grew the sun.

Now we could see the pink hearts of the lotus flowers – and so for a time the buds remained, as though waiting, flooding all the morning air with their delicate perfume. . . . Then the lances of the sun played across the roof-tops of Peking, reached westward toward the Western Hills, touching the Summer Palace in passing, and finally, as the sun rose higher and higher, covered the surface of the lake with a carpet of silver.

The sun had risen.

The miracle had happened.

For even as the sun rose, the . . . buds of lotus opened wide – and the petals spread out upon the green lotus buds as though exhausted by the ordeal of coming into life.

Her Majesty was the first to see the two white blossoms in among the pink. The white lotus blossoms were very rare. She spoke softly to me, and there was deep feeling in her voice . . . 'We shall pluck the white blossoms', she said, 'and before we have our morning repast, we shall place them in vases before Kwan Yin, the goddess of Mercy! Such rare beauty should be offered only to the goddess'.

I thought of the Viceroy, but resolutely put him out of my mind and watched the eunuchs pluck the white blossoms for Her Majesty to offer to Kwan Yin, gentle Goddess of Mercy.

I believe there are no pet dogs in China now – 'those parasitic luxuries'. Of course it is not sense to feed a dog when people are hungry and yet . . . the Chinese Republic recently destroyed the sparrows of cities and countryside because they took the grain and then discovered nature has a need of sparrows and there is need in every human being, from Empresses to paupers, for 'non-sense', play, relief. It is not sense for a tramp to share the dole of bread or meat he has been given with his dog: for an old woman on a meagre pension to spend money on seed and toys for her budgerigar, but often it is the poor who know best the value of innocent company, gaiety, colour and interest.

In old China, dogs were kept for what they were intended, either for use, hunting, guard and sheep dogs, or for pleasure; yet, without the spur of showing, the skill and the work of dedicated pekingese lovers like the Ashton Crosses of Alderbourne, we should not have the pekingese of today, far more beautiful and hardy than the original Chinese. They are a triumph of cultivation; the gardeners of the Summer Palace who curled the chrysanthemum petals and gently coaxed the paeony buds into full flower would have understood.

Queen Victoria died in 1901. The Empress Tzŭ-hsi mounted the phoenix chariot in 1908.

Both Empresses had been better loved as they grew older, the longer they ruled the more venerated they became. 'Well done, old girl', was shouted at Queen Victoria at her Diamond Jubilee. She took it as a compliment which the Empress Tzŭ-hsi would not have done though she liked to be addressed as 'Old Buddha' or 'Old Ancestor'. As time went on a stream of titles was added to her first two; in all she gathered sixteen: first Motherly and Auspicious; then Orthodox; Heaven-Blessed; Prosperous; All Nourishing; Brightly Manifest; Calm; Sedate; Perfect; Long-Lived; Respectful; Revered; Worshipful; Illustrious. She 'modestly and virtuously' declined four more with which the Emperor Kuang-hsü (not unprompted) desired to honour her, but at the very last she was given another: 'Empress Grand Dowager'. These may sound to us mere words and phrases but one must remember that each new title brought with it an income of 100,000 taels – about £30,000 a year!

Two days before Queen Victoria died, she asked, in the early hours of the morning, if she were not a little better.

'Yes.'

'Then may I have Turi?'

Over and over again we read how a pekingese will stay close to their master and mistress as they lie dying and even when they have died; but Turi was a pomeranian and, like most animals, afraid of death. He was brought and 'lay unwillingly for a short time on the bed', then presumably escaped. That is the last we hear of Queen Victoria's dogs.

There was nothing she had liked more in her life than arranging a funeral and her orders for her own were meticulously carried out.

Her little silver crucifix from above her bed was put into her hands; spring flowers were sprinkled on her white dress; her lace wedding-veil covered her face and her white widow's cap her hair. For ten days she lay in State at Osborne House . . . the crimson velvet of her robes and the diamonds of her Imperial Crown placed on the coffin . . . people knelt in the fields as the train carrying her to Windsor passed. Five Kings rode behind her as the gun carriage made its way to St George's Chapel in the Castle. There was a salute of eighty-one guns, one for each year of her life.

The Empress Tzŭ-hsi's funeral was even more gorgeous; though there were no other 'royals', unless one counts the Dalai Lama, missions were sent from all over Asia. The procession was taken through the countryside for four days, with thousands of eunuchs dressed in white, priests in saffron, camels, Manchu cavalry with their coloured banners flying, everyone garlanded with flowers, those on foot walking under state umbrellas, while the people lit paper money, paper attendants, paper food and paper clothes so that their Empress would have everything she needed in the spirit world.

Li Lien-ying, old and weary, walked before the bier with the Empress's favourite dog, Moo-tan (Paeony) a yellow and white pekingese with a white spot on its forehead, successor to the old Hai Lung. This was following precedent because the hai-pah dog, Peach Flower of the Sung Dynasty had also followed his master to the Imperial tomb and when, soon, it died of grief, it was wrapped in the cloth of an Imperial umbrella, as Confucius had recommended, and was buried beside the Emperor.

There was no Imperial umbrella for Lootie. When Dash, Queen Victoria's spaniel, died, he was buried under a marble replica of himself; all the Queen's personal pets were sculptured in life-like postures on their graves and these can be seen dotted about the private park in Windsor, but Lootie's grave is unmarked. We only know she lies near the site of the kennels, perhaps under the elms; no one, in 1872, had any idea of the future that awaited the 'golden-coated nimble dogs', her kin.

The spirit lion is, of course, immortal; butterflies are spirits too, though transient ones, in symbolism, psyches – souls after death waiting for 'orders' whether for reincarnations or to flit into heaven; it is because of this uncertainty that the butterfly cannot settle but has to flutter its wings.

We, in the world, do not know either where we are going or what we shall be; sometimes we do not even know what we are now, as with the poet Chuang Tzu, who dreamt he was a butterfly:

> Suddenly I awakened and there I lay myself again. Now I do not know whether I was then a man dreaming I was a butterfly or whether I am now a butterfly dreaming I am a man.

The pekingese is in no such dilemma; it is a butterfly *and* a lion; in fact itself – a pekingese.

The differences between the two principal breeding associations

PEKINGESE CLUB	Points	PEKIN PALACE DOG ASSOCIATION	Points
Head Massive, broad skull, wide and flat between the ears (not dome-shaped), wide between the eyes	10	*Head* Massive, broad skull, wide and flat between the ears, wide between the eyes	
Nose Black, broad, very short and flat	5	*Nose* Black, broad, very short and flat	
Eyes Large, dark, prominent, round, lustrous	5	*Eyes* Large, dark, round and lustrous	
Ears Heart shaped, not set too high, leather never long enough to come below the muzzle, not carried erect, but rather drooping, long feather	5	*Ears* Long and drooping, leather not to reach below the muzzle; long feather	25
Stop Deep	5		
Muzzle Very short and broad, not under-hung nor pointed, wrinkled	5	*Muzzle* Wrinkled and very short and broad, with level mouth; muzzle preferably black, except in black and tans and parti-colours	
Shape of Body Heavy in front, broad chest falling away lighter behind, lion-like; not too long in body	10	*Shape of Body* Broad, deep chest; body light in loins; lion-like; not long in body. Due allowance should be made for the natural difference in shape between dog and bitch in regard to lightness of loin	20
Legs Short; forelegs heavy, bowed out at elbows; hind legs lighter, but firm and well shaped	5	*Legs* Short; forelegs heavy; bowed out at elbows; hind legs lighter, but firm and well shaped	15
Feet Flat, not round; should stand well up on toes, not on ankles	5	*Feet* Flat, toes turned outwards; toes should be feathered	

<table>
<tr><td colspan="2">

Coat and Feather and Condition
Long, with thick undercoat, straight and flat not curly nor wavy; rather coarse, but soft feather on thighs, legs tail and toes, long and profuse   10

</td></tr>
</table>

Coat and Feather and Condition
Long, with thick undercoat, straight and flat not curly nor wavy; rather coarse, but soft feather on thighs, legs tail and toes, long and profuse   10

Mane
Profuse, extending beyond the shoulder blades, forming ruff or frill round front of neck   5

Tail
Curled and carried well up on loins; long profuse straight feather

Size
Being a toy dog, the smaller the better, provided type and points are not sacrificed. When divided by weight, classes should be over 10 lb and under 10 lb   5

Colour
All colours are allowable—red, fawn, black, black and tan, sable, brindle, white and parti-coloured. Black masks, and spectacles round eyes, with lines to ears, are desirable   5

Action
Free, strong and high; crossing the feet or throwing them out in running should not take off marks. Weakness of joints should be penalised   10

General Appearance
Dignity, carriage, good health   10

    100

Coat and Feather
Long, with thick undercoat, straight and soft, not curly nor wavy; feather on thighs and legs long and profuse

Mane
Profuse and coarser than the rest of coat   } 15

Tail
Carried high on loins in a loose curl; long, profuse straight feather

Size
Maximum weight 10 lb; minimum weight 5 lb   } 5

Colour
All colours are allowable. In particolours the colour must be evenly broken. The Association does not recognise what is known as liver-coloured dogs

Action
Free, strong and high   10

General Appearance
Dignity, carriage, good health   10

    100

Disqualifications
Blindness, if total; docked tail; cropped ears

Penalizations
Paralysed tongue; the loss of one eye; blemished eye.

— and a thousand for expression

Acknowledgements

I AM GRATEFUL to the experts who have answered my queries, from whose books I have profited by reading, and who have allowed me to quote from some of these, especially to Elizabeth Longford, Marina Warner and Ellic Howe. In some cases the most strenuous enquiries have failed to trace the copyright owners of long out-of-print works and I hope that they will, if they see this book, forgive me and accept my assurance that an acknowledgement will appear in any reprinted edition if they care to write to me, or to my publishers. Source notes for quoted passages will be found on pages 183–7.

I am indebted to Clifford Hubbard, the authority on 'dog' books for his help and to Miss Cynthia Ashton Cross for making available to me the records of the Alderbourne Kennels and for the loan of rare books.

I am more than grateful to my devoted research workers Elizabeth Kirwan-Taylor in England, Eleanor Wolquitt in New York and Betty MacRae in Toronto for undertaking the arduous work of tracking down illustrations for me, often from relatively obscure sources. I thank Theo Townshend for the permission to reproduce her collage: Vaughan Kimber and Francis Pilgrim for the care and skill they devoted to photographs taken specially for this book; and to the staffs of museums all over the world for their help and encouragement.

List of illustrations

Decorations in the text are by Caroline Garnham.

87 White paeony, 10th–11th century. (Nelson–Atkins Gallery, Kansas City, Missouri)

88 Ch'ien-lung composing verses in his garden. (Peking Palace Museum)

93 The entry of Lord Elgin into Peking on 24 October 1860. (Reproduced from *The Great Within* by Maurice Collis)

105 Queen Victoria in middle age, painted by Lady Abercrombie. (National Portrait Gallery, London)

107 Tzŭ-hsi painted by the American artist Katharine Carl. (The Smithsonian Institution, Freer Gallery of Art, Washington, D.C.)

110 The winter crown and jewelled nail protectors. (National Palace Museum, Taipei, Taiwan)

113 Balmoral Castle. (Radio Times Hulton Picture Library)

115 Chrysanthemum scroll on silk. (National Palace Museum, Taipei, Taiwan)

125 Snuff bottle in amber and agate, 18th–19th century. (Victoria and Albert Museum, photograph AVK)

127 Court lady with a dog: reverse of a hand-mirror. (Reproduced from Collier)

131 Pekingese painted by Tsugouhara Foujita. (Weyhe Gallery, New York)

133 Ivory of a pekingese with a butterfly. Japan *c.* 1820. (Reproduced by courtesy of Mallett of Bourdon House Limited)

139 Dogs playing. (*Royal Favourites*, Koehn)

141 Lord John Hay and Schlorff in the 1860s. (Reproduced from *The Pekingese Scrapbook*, Elsa and Ellic Howe)

146 Screen painted by Maud Earl. (Private collection, England)

Source Notes

My chief source of information was V. W. F. Collier's book, *Dogs of China and Japan in Nature and Art*. Messrs. Heinemann's records of him were destroyed in the Second World War and we have only been able to trace that he was, in reality, William Collins, lived in China and obviously spoke Chinese.

Scholar as he was, V. W. F. Collier gives, in almost every case, the sources of his quotations, almost all Chinese, but as these books are for the most part in Peking and the Chinese authorities are not interested in the history of 'non-utility' dogs, regarding them as frivolities — as they are — it has proved impossible to check these references.

Figures before italicised catch-phrases are page numbers. References to books included in the general Bibliography (page 188) are given in shortened form. All quotations from letters and diaries of Queen Victoria and the Prince Consort are taken from the standard published sources.

CHAPTER ONE '*Golden-coated nimble dogs*'

Page

16 *Captain 99th Regiment.* Unpublished correspondence in the Royal Archives, Windsor, here and subsequently quoted by gracious permission of Her Majesty the Queen.

38 *had his lion* Vlasto, *Through Chinese Spectacles.*

40 *upon his back* Collier.

All otherwise unattributed quotations in this chapter are from Collier.

CHAPTER TWO Empresses-in-Waiting.

44 *they have ever seen* Dunne.
44 *about its treatment* unpublished correspondence in the Royal Archives, Windsor.
47 *the Son of Heaven* Varè.
49 *the famous words 'I will be good'* Woodham-Smith.
53 *bowed with blossom* Warner.
54 *and pluck an empty twig* adapted from *Gold-Thread Coat* by Tu Ch'iu (9th century) translated by Robert Kotewall and Norman L. Smith and included in *The Penguin Book of Chinese Verse*.
57 Account of Emperor's dissipation derived from Timothy Richard, *Forty-five Years in China* (1916), quoted in Warner.
59 *without our knowledge* quoted in Watson.
59 *food for it* unpublished correspondence in the Royal Archives, Windsor.
61 *that is good for him* ibid.
64 *warned in time* quoted in Waley.

CHAPTER THREE The Flower that made a War

66 *the hour of the rat* Cronin.
68 *orchards of England* Graham.
71 *without noticing them* Hans Andersen, *The Nightingale*.
72 *'I protest' says the lady* . . . Oliver Goldsmith, *The Citizen of the World* (republished in 1762, having previously appeared as *Chinese Letters*, by John Newbery in his *Public Ledger*, and quoted in Honour, *Chinoiserie*).
74 *belonging to the court* Collier.
74 *his only ornament* Collis, *Foreign Mud*.
76 *indeed OUR vassal* ibid.

79 *among the crew* article in *The Yachtsman*, quoted in Collis, *Foreign Mud*.

80 *or dreamful ease* 'Choric Song' from Tennyson, 'The Lotos-Eaters'.

80 *lend ourselves to this traffic* A. S. Thelwall, *The Iniquities of the Opium Trade with China* London 1839.

81 *set foot upon your shores* Waley.

82 *live to reach England* quoted in Steele.

86 *Nine Islands* Graham.

88 *cut in stone* ibid.

89 *ordinary forage cap* Wolseley.

89 *hold the reins* ibid.

90 *looked directly at it* Rev. R. J. L. M'Ghee, Chaplain to the Forces, *How we got to Peking* 1862.

91 *over his delicate hands* Robert Swinhoe, *Narrative of the North China Campaign of 1860*, London 1861.

92 *endless sorrow flows* 68 'P'u-Nien Nu Chiao' (rendered into verse by Alan Ayling from translations by Duncan Mackintosh) *A Collection of Chinese Lyrics*, Routledge and Kegan Paul, 1965.

93 *bands playing* Wolseley.

96 *specimens were imported* Rennie.

96 *seen by Her Majesty* unpublished correspondence in the Royal Archives, Windsor.

97 *in Her room* ibid.

97 *its own merits* ibid.

97 *it will die* ibid.

97 *or a Court lady* ibid.

98 *heart to rest* lines in memory of Li-Fu-Jen, Concubine of the Emperor Wu, probably written 700 or 600 B.C. and translated by Arthur Waley.

CHAPTER FOUR *The Winter Castle and the Summer Palace.*

100 *bright red silk* Der-ling, *Imperial Incense.*

101 *routine of the court* ibid.

102 *put it down* Carl.

104 *and eventful as mine* Der-ling, *Imperial Incense.*

104 *I must decide myself* ibid.

111 *to offer them* quoted in Watson.

111 *two jade clasps* Der-ling, *Imperial Incense.*

111 *of several villages* Satire by Chen Yun Sou, quoted in *The Four Seasons of T'ang Poetry* by John H. C. Wu, Charles Tuttle Co, 1972.

112 *duty and truth* Prodan.

112 *wonderfully beautiful* and succeeding quotations, Queen Victoria, *Our Life in the Highlands.*

114 *has no heart* Der-ling, *Imperial Incense.*

114 account of Tzŭ-hsi's building activities derived from Warner.

115 *had been sacrificed* Graham.

116 *wore jet and hardly uttered* Mallet.

118 *after dinner* Longford.

121 *dog had to be taken away* Der-ling, *Imperial Incense.*

121 *interesting little animals* Carl.

124 *her dear hands* Mallet.

CHAPTER FIVE *Points and Pearls*

126–9 The Pearls. These 'Pearls' are quoted in roughly the same form in every book about pekingese—except in V. W. F. Collier's. But see page 130.

130 *in her hands* Der-ling, *Imperial Incense.*

130 *matters of state* ibid.

132 *copies of . . .* Howe.

134 *for several days* and unattributed quotations pp 132–139, quoted in Collier.
135 *effect in sunlight* Vlasto.
135 *chest and paws* Ashton Cross.
136 *of the eyes* Collier.
137 *of some Bull-dogs* J. E. Gray, F.R.S. 'On the skull of the Chinese pug-nosed spaniel or lap-dog', Proceedings of the Zoological Society, 1867.
141 *said with pride and pleasure* Mrs Archibald Little, *Intimate China* 1899.
144 *presented him to me* Carl.
145 *beautiful puppies* Der-ling *Imperial Incense*.

CHAPTER SIX *The Alderbournes*

Nearly all the material for this chapter comes from the unpublished records of the Alderbourne Kennels, Ascot, Berkshire, from Mrs Ashton Cross's standard work *The Pekingese Dog* (1932) and from personal conversations and correspondence I have had with her daughters.
171 *gentle Goddess of Mercy* Der-ling, *Imperial Incense*.

EPILOGUE

172 Account of the Dowager Empress's titles derived from Bland and Backhouse – not, as Professor Trevor-Roper in *A Hidden Life*, 1976, has shown, a wholly reputable source.
173 *year of her life* Longford.
174 *dreaming I am a man* quoted by Margaret R. Thiele in *None but the Nightingale* Charles Tuttle Co, 1967.

Bibliography

Allen, Minna Loftus, *Show Pekingese* (n.d.).

Bland, J. O. P. and Backhouse, E., *China under the Empress Dowager* (Heinemann, 1910).

Buck, Pearl S., *Imperial Woman* (Methuen, 1956).

Carl, Katharine, *With the Empress Dowager of China* (1906).

Chinese Classics. The Four Books; Confucian Analects, Great Learning, Doctrine of the Mean, Works of Mencius, And the Work of Lao-Tsze, ed. and trans. J. Legge (Kegan Paul, Trench, Trubner, n.d.).

Collier, V. W. F., *Dogs of China and Japan in Nature and Art* (Heinemann, 1921).

Collis, Maurice, *Foreign Mud* (Faber, 1946).

——, *The Great Within* (Faber, 1941).

——, *The Motherly and Auspicious* (Faber, 1943).

Cronin, Vincent, *The Wise Man from the West* (Hart-Davis, 1955).

Cross, Mrs Ashton, *The Pekingese Dog* (1932).

Dale-Green, Patricia, *Dog* (Hart-Davis, 1966).

Danby, Hope, *The Garden of Perfect Brightness* (Williams & Norgate, 1950).

Der-ling, Princess, *Imperial Incense* (Stanley Paul & Co, n.d.).

——, *Two Years in the Forbidden City* (Fisher Unwin, 1912).

Dickinson, G. Lowes, *Letters from John Chinaman and Other Essays* (Allen & Unwin, 1946).

Dixey, Annie Coath, *The Lion Dog of Peking* (Peter Davies, 1931).

Duff, David, *Albert and Victoria* (Muller, 1972).

Dunne, J. H., *From Calcutta to Pekin* (Sampson, Low, 1861).

Edwards, E. D., *The Dragon Book* (William Hodge, 1938).

Fisher, M. F. K., *Here Let Us Feast* (New York : Viking Press, 1946).

Four Seasons of T'ang Poetry, ed. John C. H. Wu (Rutland, Vt : Charles E. Tuttle, 1972).

Francis, William, *Portrait of a Queen* (French, 1966).

Gorst, Harold E., *China* (n.d.).

Graham, Dorothy, *Chinese Gardens* (Harrap, 1938).

Hibbert, Christopher, *The Dragon Wakes: China and the West, 1793–1911* (Longman, 1970).

Hirth, Friedrich, *The Ancient History of China* (New York, 1923).

Honour, Hugh, *Chinoiserie* (John Murray, 1961).

Howe, Elsa and Ellic, *The Pekingese Scrapbook* (Chapman & Hall, 1954).

Hubbard, C. L. B., *The Pekingese Handbook* (Nicholson & Watson, 1951).

A Hundred and Seventy Chinese Poems, trans. Arthur Waley (Constable, 1918).

Inglis, Brian, *The Opium War* (Hodder & Stoughton, 1976).

Johnson, Rowland, *Our Friend the Pekingese* (Methuen, 1932).

Koehn, Alfred, *Royal Favourites* (Peiping, 1948).

Leighton, Robert, *The Complete Book of the Dog* (Cassell, 1922).

Lin Yutang, *Imperial Peking* (Elek, 1961).

Longford, Elizabeth, *Victoria R.I.* (Weidenfeld & Nicholson, 1964).

Love and Protest: Chinese poems from the 6th century B.C. *to the 17th century* A.D. (n.d.).

Lytton, Lady, *Lady Lytton's Diary* (n.d.).

Mallet, Victor, *Life with Queen Victoria* (John Murray, 1963).

Polo, Marco, *The Travels of Marco Polo*, Everyman's Library (Dent, 1908).

Prodan, Mario, *Chinese Art* (Hutchinson, 1958).

Rennie, D. F. *Peking and the Pekingese* (1865).

Scidmore, E. R., *China the Long-Lived Empire* (Macmillan, 1900).

Selby, John, *The Paper Dragon: an account of the China Wars. 1840–1900* (Arthur Barker, 1968).

Smythe, Lillian, *The Pekingese* (The Kennel, n.d.).

Steele, Queenie Verity, *The Book on Pekingese* (n.d.).

Strachey, Lytton, *Queen Victoria* (Chatto & (Windus, 1921).

Tu Fu, *Selected Poems* (Commercial Press, n.d.).

Tzu Yeh, *Love Poems of Tzu Yeh* (Gold Orchid, n.d.).

Varè, Daniele, *The Last of the Empresses* (John Murray, 1936).

Victoria, Queen, *Leaves from the Journal of Our Life in the Highlands, 1848–61.* ed. A. Helps (1868).

Vlasto, John A., *The Popular Pekingese* (Popular Dogs Publishing Co, 1935).

——, '*Through Chinese Spectacles, being the Testament of Lo-li, a Pekingese Lion Dog*' (unpublished).

Waley, Arthur, *The Opium War through Chinese Eyes* (Allen & Unwin, 1958).

Warner, Marina, *The Dragon Empress: life and times of Tz'u-hsi, 1835–1908* (Weidenfeld & Nicolson, 1972).

Watson, Vera, *A Queen at Home* (W. H. Allen, 1952).

Wolseley, G. J. (Viscount) *Narrative of the China War* (1862).

Woodham-Smith, Cecil, *Queen Victoria: her life and times*, vol. 1, *1819–61* (Hamish Hamilton, 1972).

Your Dear Letter: private correspondence of Queen Victoria and the Crown Princess of Prussia, 1865–71, ed. Roger Fulford (Evans, 1971).

Index

Numbers in italics refer to illustrations